bills food

For Natalie and Edie

A book is not just the work of one person, but the work of a number of talented people, not unlike a restaurant! So I'd like to take this opportunity to thank Kay, for her patience, enthusiasm, support and vision. Thanks to Petrina, Kristen and Briget for making the food come alive with the most beautiful photographs; Marylouise for her design and patience with my input; Jane and Lulu for their food editing; Vanessa Broadfoot, Rebecca Clancy, Kathleen Gandy, Jo Glynn and Christine Osmond for their rigorous testing, making sure these recipes work at home; Sophie, Andy, Kath and Nicole for running the restaurants while I did the book; Anna and Peter Schutzinger for the use of their beautiful house and finally, Natalie, for without her nothing would happen!

This edition first published in Canada by Whitecap Books, 351 Lynn Ave., North Vancouver, BC V7J 2C4.

Published by Murdoch Books®, a division of Murdoch Magazines Pty Ltd.

The publisher would like to thank the following for their generosity in supplying props and kitchenware for this book: AEG Kitchen Appliances; All Hand Made, Bison, Breville Holdings Pty Ltd, Chief Australia, Sara de Nardi (for beautiful napery), Design Mode International, Empire Homeware, Simon Johnson, Kitchen Aid, Koskela, Orrefors Kosta Boda, Orson & Blake, Papaya, Peppergreen Antiques, Planet Furniture, Poliform, Roylston House, Space Furniture, Spence & Lyda. Thanks also for fashion to Marcs, Robby Ingham.

Chief Executive: Juliet Rogers

Publisher: Kay Scarlett

Production Manager: Kylie Kirkwood

Art Direction and Design: Marylouise Brammer; Photographer: Petrina Tinslay;
Editorial Director: Diana Hill; Editor: Wendy Stephen; Food Editors: Jane Lawson, Lulu Grimes;
Props and Food Stylist: Kristen Anderson; Home Economist: Briget Palmer.

Printed by Toppan Printing Hong Kong Co. Ltd. PRINTED IN CHINA

ISBN 1 55285 436 1

bills food

by bill granger

photography by petrina tinslay

whitecap

contents

'This is the food I like to cook now. Quick, easy, nourishing and comforting, it reflects this time in my life. It's not necessarily complicated but is the food I'm increasingly drawn towards and find myself wanting to cook. I cook this food for my family and for my friends.

As I get older and my life becomes busier with work and family, the time available to prepare and cook meals gets shorter. But being busier actually increases the desire to spend time connecting with home. Food's a big part of that.

Food is such a simple pleasure and preparing it gives a sense of calm, time to stop. After a big day the temptation is often there to call for home delivery but, if I think before dialling, I invariably realize I'd rather have something healthier and lighter, home-made and wholesome.

An empty fridge and pantry can be very uninspiring and a full fridge can be unrealistic if you're working a lot and eating out every second night. However, if you always have pantry staples such as tuna, rice and canned tomatoes, you can make a quick, delicious meal. At the end of the week, unused vegetables can be made into a hearty soup to freeze.

The ability to create food is one of life's most reassuring skills and is immensely satisfying. I hope these recipes inspire you.'

Bill

breakfast

breakfast

'I love cooking breakfast. Few people have the time to prepare a complete breakfast at home, but everyone appreciates it when someone does it for them. These days I love inviting people home for breakfast and I try to make a special effort for my family. As long as it's fresh, it doesn't matter what you serve but I always include a plate of fresh fruit. Everyone loves a pancake, whether it's sweet or savoury, and a big deep omelette is great to serve a crowd. Most of all, breakfast should be lazy. I always find making toast for lots of people is too hard so I just buy a fresh loaf and serve it untoasted. And don't attempt to make espresso coffee for everyone — leave that to the professionals — plunger coffee is just fine. Relax, just pop the food and a big jug of juice in the middle of the table and let people help themselves. Remember, you are not a restaurant — and it's all about the company after all!'

To caramelize plums, heat a frying pan over a high heat, cut the plums in half, sprinkle the cut sides with sugar and put the plums in a hot frying pan with the cut side down. Sear the plums until the sugar melts and caramelizes. This should take about a minute.

buttermilk pancakes

250 g (2 cups) plain (all-purpose) flour
3 teaspoons baking powder
a pinch of salt
2 tablespoons sugar
2 eggs, lightly beaten
750 ml (3 cups) buttermilk
75 g (2^1/$_2$ oz) unsalted butter, melted
unsalted butter, extra, for greasing the pan

to serve
caramelized plums (see above)
maple syrup
yoghurt

Stir the flour, baking powder, salt and sugar together in a bowl. Add the eggs, buttermilk and melted butter and whisk to combine.

Heat a large non-stick frying pan over a medium heat and brush a small portion of butter over the base. For each pancake, ladle 80 ml (1/3 cup) of batter into the pan and cook for about 2 minutes, until bubbles appear on the surface. Turn the pancakes over and cook for another minute. Transfer to a plate and keep warm while cooking the rest of the pancakes.

Serve the pancakes in stacks with the plums, a jug of maple syrup and some yoghurt. Makes 16

You can, of course, use other kinds of soft cheese in this recipe. Choose something which will melt easily. I've often used ricotta or grated Emmenthal.

omelette with goat's curd and sage

3 eggs
1 teaspoon butter, for greasing the pan
85 g (3 oz) goat's curd
1 tablespoon fresh sage leaves
sea salt
freshly ground black pepper

Break the eggs into a medium bowl, add 1 tablespoon water and beat lightly with a fork until just combined.

Heat a non-stick frying pan over a medium to high heat. Add the butter and swirl to coat the base of the pan. Pour in the beaten eggs and, as the eggs begin to cook, use a wooden spoon to carefully drag the cooked egg to the centre, allowing the uncooked mixture to flow towards the edges. Repeat a second time (this will only take a minute). When the omelette is nearly cooked (the eggs are still wet on the top), add the goat's curd and sage leaves in a line down the centre. Season with salt and pepper, then fold the sides of the omelette over the filling. Slide out onto a plate and serve with fresh crusty bread. Serves 1

When mixing batters, you will often see the words 'do not overmix'. This is so you don't work the gluten in the flour and toughen the mixture as this makes the end result tough and dry. A loose mixture ensures a moist and delicious result.

choc banana bread

250 g (2 cups) plain (all-purpose) flour
2 teaspoons baking powder
125 g (4$^{1}/_{2}$ oz) unsalted butter, softened
250 g (1 cup) caster (superfine) sugar
4 ripe bananas, mashed
2 eggs, lightly beaten
1 teaspoon vanilla extract
175 g (1 cup) good-quality dark or milk chocolate chips

Preheat the oven to 180°C (350°F/Gas 4). Sift the flour and baking powder into a large bowl.

Mix the butter, sugar, banana, eggs, vanilla extract and chocolate chips in a separate bowl. Add to the dry ingredients and stir to combine, being careful not to overmix.

Pour the batter into a non-stick, or lightly greased and floured, 19 x 11 cm (7$^{1}/_{2}$ x 4$^{1}/_{2}$ inch) loaf tin and bake for 1 hour 15 minutes, or until the bread is cooked when tested with a skewer. Leave to cool in the tin for 5 minutes before turning out onto a wire rack to cool. Serve in thick slices with butter. Makes 8 to 10 slices

potato cakes with smoked salmon and mustard dressing

3 large potatoes (about 700 g/1 lb 9 oz in total)
2 tablespoons chopped fresh chives
60 g ($2^{1}/4$ oz) butter, melted
sea salt
freshly ground black pepper
60 ml ($1/4$ cup) olive oil

to serve
8 slices smoked salmon
mustard dressing (below)

Preheat the oven to 150°C (300°F/Gas 2). Grate the peeled potatoes and squeeze out any excess liquid. Put the potato in a bowl and add the chives, melted butter and a little salt and pepper.

Heat the oil in a large non-stick pan over a medium to high heat. For each potato cake, spoon $1^{1}/2$ tablespoons of mixture into the pan and fry until golden on both sides. Drain on paper towels and keep warm in the oven until all the potato cakes are made.

Put two potato cakes on each plate, top with the salmon and drizzle with mustard dressing. You can garnish with sprigs of fresh herbs if you wish. Serves 4

mustard dressing

2 teaspoons Dijon mustard
2 teaspoons sugar
$1/2$ teaspoon salt
1 tablespoon white wine vinegar
60 ml ($1/4$ cup) canola oil

Whisk the mustard, sugar, salt and vinegar together in a bowl until the sugar has dissolved, then whisk in the oil in a thin stream.

Mushrooms keep best if you store them in a brown paper bag to allow them to breathe. Keeping them in plastic causes them to sweat and go slimy.

mushrooms on toast

40 g (1^1/$_2$ oz) unsalted butter
1 tablespoon olive oil, plus extra, for brushing
2 garlic cloves, finely chopped
500 g (1 lb 2 oz) mixed small mushrooms such as button and Swiss brown
sea salt
freshly ground black pepper
1 teaspoon balsamic vinegar
2 tablespoons chopped fresh flat-leaf parsley
1 teaspoon chopped fresh tarragon
1 teaspoon grated lemon zest
4 slices sourdough bread
1 garlic clove, extra, for rubbing on bread
250 g (1 cup) ricotta cheese

Put half the butter with the oil and chopped garlic in a saucepan over a medium to high heat. Add the mushrooms, 60 ml (^{1}/$_4$ cup) water and salt and pepper, to taste. Cover and cook, stirring occasionally, for about 15 minutes, or until the mushrooms are cooked and the liquid is syrupy. Stir in the balsamic vinegar, parsley, tarragon and lemon zest. Taste for seasoning and adjust if necessary. Whisk the remaining cold butter through to thicken the mushroom sauce.

Brush the bread on both sides with the extra olive oil. Grill until golden on both sides, then rub both sides with a cut garlic clove and place on serving plates. Top with ricotta and then mushrooms and serve immediately. Serves 4

crepes with ricotta filling and bitter orange sauce

crepes
90 g (3/4 cup) plain (all-purpose) flour
1 egg, lightly beaten
250 ml (1 cup) milk
20 g (3/4 oz) butter, melted
a pinch of salt
extra butter, for greasing the pan

filling
2 tablespoons milk
2 tablespoons sultanas
250 g (1 cup) ricotta cheese
1 teaspoon grated lemon zest
1 1/2 teaspoons icing (confectioners') sugar
1/2 teaspoon vanilla extract

to serve
icing (confectioners') sugar, for dusting
bitter orange sauce (below)

To prepare the crepes, put the flour in a large bowl, add the egg, milk, melted butter and salt and whisk until smooth. Refrigerate for 2 hours before cooking.

While the crepe batter is resting, prepare the filling by heating the milk and sultanas in a small saucepan over a low heat for 2 to 3 minutes. Remove from the heat and allow to cool for 5 minutes. Transfer the milk and sultanas to a bowl, add the ricotta, lemon zest, icing sugar and vanilla extract and stir to combine.

Heat a non-stick frying pan over a medium heat and brush a little butter over the base. Ladle 2 tablespoons of batter into the pan and tip the pan slightly to quickly and evenly spread the batter. After a minute, lift the outer edge of the crepe and flip it over and cook for a couple of seconds on the other side. Repeat with the remaining batter.

Place a heaped tablespoon of filling in the centre of each crepe. Fold the crepe into quarters (crepes can be made in advance to this stage). Heat a non-stick frying pan over a medium heat and brush with butter. Put the filled and folded crepes into the pan and cook for about 30 seconds on each side. Place two crepes on each serving plate, dust with icing sugar and drizzle with sauce. Serves 4

bitter orange sauce

80 g (1/4 cup) good-quality orange marmalade
60 ml (1/4 cup) orange juice
1 tablespoon brandy or Grand Marnier (optional)

Put the marmalade, orange juice and brandy or Grand Marnier, if using, in a small saucepan over a low heat and stir until the marmalade has melted.

Cutting a cross in the skin of the peach will make it much easier to peel back the skin after cooking.

white peaches in rose-water syrup

500 g (1 lb 2 oz) caster (superfine) sugar
1 tablespoon rose-water
4 white peaches

to serve
plain yoghurt (optional)
90 g (^{2}/$_3$ cup) chopped pistachios

Put the caster sugar and rose-water into a saucepan with 1 litre (4 cups) of water and bring it to the boil. Cut a small cross in the skin at the top of each peach with a sharp knife, then add the peaches to the saucepan and gently simmer for 5 minutes, or until tender. Take the peaches out of the syrup and slip off the skins. Put the skins back into the syrup and cook for 10 minutes, or until the syrup has reduced by half. Strain the syrup and cool.

Serve the peaches with some syrup, a dollop of yoghurt, if you like, and a sprinkling of chopped pistachios. Serves 4

french toast with fresh berry sauce

3 eggs
185 ml (3/4 cup) milk
8 thick slices brioche or panettone
30 g (1 oz) unsalted butter

to serve
fresh berry sauce (below)
icing (confectioners') sugar, for sprinkling

Whisk the eggs and milk together in a bowl to combine. Place the brioche or panettone in a shallow dish and pour the milk mixture over the top. Allow the milk to soak in thoroughly, then turn the bread over and soak the other side — if you are using panettone it will need to be soaked for a little longer because it is drier.

Heat a large non-stick frying pan over a medium to high heat and melt half of the butter. Add four slices of bread to the pan and fry for about 1 minute, until golden. Turn over and cook until the other side is golden. Repeat with the remaining bread.

Serve immediately with berry sauce and a sprinkling of icing sugar. Serves 4

fresh berry sauce

250 g (2 cups) raspberries or mixed berries
60 g (1/4 cup) caster (superfine) sugar
1 tablespoon lemon juice

Put half the berries in a blender with the sugar and lemon juice. Purée until smooth, then pour into a bowl, add the remaining berries and stir to combine.

If you can't get cherry tomatoes, just cut ordinary tomatoes into eight, drizzle them with olive oil, sprinkle them with a little oregano, salt and pepper and bake at 200°C (400°F/Gas 6) for 20 to 25 minutes.

open-faced feta and leek omelette

2 tablespoons olive oil
2 leeks, washed and sliced, white part only
sea salt
freshly ground black pepper
3 small zucchini (courgettes), finely sliced
2 tablespoons chopped fresh mint
3 tablespoons chopped fresh flat-leaf (Italian) parsley
6 eggs, lightly beaten with 2 tablespoons water
115 g (4 oz) feta, drained

to serve
60 ml (1/4 cup) olive oil
a few fresh oregano leaves
16 baby vine-ripened tomatoes on their stalks
extra virgin olive oil, for drizzling

Heat the grill to its highest setting. Place a 22 cm (9 inch) non-stick frying pan (with a heatproof handle) over a medium to high heat. Add the olive oil, leek, salt and pepper and cook for 5 minutes, stirring occasionally. Add the zucchini and cook for another 5 minutes. Sprinkle with the herbs and pour the eggs over the top. Crumble the feta over the omelette and cook for 5 minutes. Finish under the grill for another 5 minutes, or until golden and bubbling.

Heat the olive oil in a saucepan, add the oregano and tomatoes and toss them in the hot oil until they just start to soften and split. Season with salt and black pepper.

Serve wedges of omelette with the tomatoes and a good drizzle of extra virgin olive oil. Serves 4

Often the first pikelet is a dud so don't be disheartened — just try again.

wholemeal pikelets with butter, lemon and sugar

125 g (1 cup) wholemeal plain (all-purpose) flour
2 teaspoons baking powder
2 tablespoons raw sugar
1 egg, lightly beaten
170 ml (2/3 cup) milk
butter, for greasing the pan

to serve
30 g (1 oz) butter
55 g (1/4 cup) raw sugar
2 lemons

Sift the flour and baking powder into a bowl. Add the sugar and stir to combine. Add the egg and milk and whisk until smooth.

Heat a large non-stick frying pan over a medium heat and brush with butter, being careful not to let the butter brown. Spoon tablespoons of mixture into the pan and cook for about 2 minutes, until bubbles appear on the surface. Turn the pikelets over and cook for another 30 seconds.

Serve hot from the pan with extra butter, a sprinkle of sugar and a squeeze of lemon. Makes 12

I always use fresh ricotta cut from the wheel whenever I can. The texture is much smoother and the flavour is better. If you have a tub of ricotta, put it in a sieve over a bowl and drain it in the fridge overnight to get rid of any excess liquid.

baked sweet ricotta with honeyed figs

750 g (1 lb 10 oz) ricotta cheese
2 eggs
45 g (1/4 cup) soft brown sugar
1 teaspoon vanilla extract

to serve
4 figs
honey
raisin toast (optional)

Preheat the oven to 180°C (350°F/Gas 4). Put the ricotta, eggs, sugar and vanilla in a bowl and mix them well. Grease four 250 ml (1 cup) muffin holes and divide the mixture among them.

Bake for 20 to 25 minutes, or until the ricotta cakes are puffed and light golden. Leave them to sit for 2 minutes before turning them out.

To serve, put each ricotta cake on a plate and add some halved figs and a drizzle of honey.
Serves 4

The quickest and easiest way to toast nuts is to dry-fry them in a frying pan over a medium heat. However, don't walk away from them because they burn very quickly.

bircher muesli with pear and blueberries

200 g (2 cups) rolled oats or mixed rolled oats, barley and rye
375 ml (1^{1}/2 cups) pear juice
2 pears, skin left on and grated
125 g (^{1}/2 cup) plain yoghurt
4 tablespoons toasted chopped almonds
80 g (^{1}/2 cup) blueberries

Put the rolled oats, barley and rye in a bowl with the pear juice and leave to soak for 1 hour, or overnight, in the fridge. Add the grated pear and yoghurt and mix well. Spoon the muesli into serving bowls and top each with toasted almonds and blueberries. Serves 4

lunch

lunch

'One of the world's best lunches is a fresh baguette with cheese. In winter however, lunch to me says soup with fresh herbs and a piece of crunchy bread. If you're entertaining at lunch, you don't need to serve a lot of different things and, although I'm constantly experimenting with new flavours and methods, there's nothing wrong with finding the things you do really well and sticking with them. One of the easiest ways to do lunch is to buy a good-quality ham and put it in the middle of the table with a basket of rolls and some chutney. Another simple option is to do a mixed plate with smoked salmon, a lentil salad and perhaps some steamed asparagus. Of course, there are no rules about lunch. Lunch can be dinner, just served in the middle of the table on platters rather than plated up. Remember that people come to see you and the most important thing is to be relaxed when entertaining. If you're relaxed, the food will be better, whereas if you're not, you and the food will be tortured.'

To segment lemons, cut slices off the top and bottom. Sit the lemon on one end and slice away the peel and pith, leaving bare flesh exposed. Cut out segments in between the membrane with a sharp knife.

rare tuna salad with fennel and lemon dressing

1 tablespoon olive oil
500 g (1 lb 2 oz) tuna, cut into large batons, roughly 5 cm (2 inches) square at the ends
1 tablespoon sea salt
freshly ground black pepper
300 g (11 oz) green beans
1 baby cos (romaine) lettuce
2 heads of witlof (chicory/Belgian endive), broken into leaves
1 baby fennel bulb, finely sliced
lemon dressing (below)

Brush the olive oil over the tuna and season with salt and pepper. Heat a large non-stick frying pan over a high heat, add the tuna and cook for 20 seconds on each side of the batons. Remove from the pan and allow to rest for up to 1 hour. Cut the tuna into 5 mm (1/4 inch) slices.

Blanch the beans in boiling water for 2 minutes, then refresh them in cold water. Arrange the cos, witlof, fennel and beans on plates, top with the tuna and spoon the lemon dresssing over the top. Serves 4

lemon dressing

1 lemon, segmented, with pith and membrane removed (see above)
3 tablespoons baby capers, rinsed
60 ml (1/4 cup) extra virgin olive oil
sea salt
freshly ground black pepper

Stir all the dressing ingredients together in a bowl and leave to rest for 10 minutes.

burger with hummus and potato wedges

4 good-quality hamburger buns or rolls
500 g (1 lb 2 oz) lean beef mince
1 red onion, grated
sea salt
freshly ground black pepper
3 tablespoons olive oil
250 g (1 punnet) cherry tomatoes, sliced
1/2 teaspoon sumac

1 small white salad onion, cut into thin
   wedges
15 g (1/4 cup) shredded fresh parsley
1 tablespoon lemon juice
hummus (below)

to serve
potato wedges (below)

Cut the buns horizontally into halves. Put the mince, onion, salt and pepper in a bowl and combine well with your hands. Form into four patties, making them slightly larger than the buns because they will shrink during cooking.

Heat 2 tablespoons of the oil in a large non-stick frying pan over a medium to high heat, add the hamburger patties and, because the patties tend to puff up, make a small dip in the centre of each with the back of a spoon. Cook for 4 minutes on each side, or until done to your liking.

Make the salad by tossing the cherry tomatoes, sumac, onion and parsley together with the remaining olive oil and the lemon juice. While the burgers are cooking, toast the buns with the cut side up. Spread hummus on the toasted sides, then top with a patty, salad and the bun tops. Serve with potato wedges. Serves 4

hummus

400 g (14 oz) can chickpeas, drained
1 garlic clove
2 tablespoons lemon juice

sea salt
freshly ground black pepper

Process the chickpeas, garlic and lemon juice in a food processor with 3 tablespoons of water until the hummus is smooth. Season, to taste, with salt and pepper.

potato wedges

1 1/2 tablespoons vegetable oil
5 garlic cloves, unpeeled and crushed with
   the side of a knife
1 1/2 tablespoons lime juice
2 teaspoons Tabasco sauce

500 g (1 lb) potatoes, unpeeled, scrubbed,
   dried and cut into wedges
freshly ground black pepper
sea salt

Preheat the oven to 200°C (400°F/Gas 6). Put the oil, garlic, lime juice and Tabasco sauce in a large bowl and whisk to combine. Add the potatoes and pepper and stir until the potatoes are coated. Transfer to a baking dish, spreading the potatoes evenly over the dish with the rounded side down. Bake for 45 minutes, or until crispy. Sprinkle with sea salt and serve.

Don't be scared to use fresh beetroot as it is
actually very easy to cook. Roasting beetroot,
rather than boiling it, intensifies its earthy flavour.

orange, beetroot and goat's curd salad

250 g (1 bunch) watercress
4 medium-sized beetroot, scrubbed
sea salt
freshly ground black pepper
200 g (7 oz) green beans
4 oranges, peeled and sliced into rounds
125 g (4^{1}/$_{2}$ oz) goat's curd or goat's cheese

dressing
125 ml (^{1}/$_{2}$ cup) extra virgin olive oil
2 tablespoons red wine vinegar

Preheat the oven to 200°C (400°F/Gas 6). Pick the tips off the watercress and discard the stalks.
Place the beetroot on a sheet of foil and sprinkle liberally with salt and pepper. Wrap them
securely in the foil, place on a baking tray and bake for 1^{1}/$_{2}$ to 2 hours, or until the beetroot
is tender when pierced with a skewer. Allow the beetroot to cool, then cut each beetroot into
eight wedges.

Blanch the beans in boiling water for 2 minutes, then refresh them in cold water and slice each
in half lengthways.

Whisk the olive oil and vinegar and some salt and pepper together in a small bowl until
combined. Divide the orange slices, green beans, beetroot and watercress among four plates
and add 1 heaped tablespoon of goat's curd per serving. Drizzle with dressing and serve.
Serves 4

poached chicken and asparagus salad

3 fresh flat-leaf (Italian) parsley stems
1 tablespoon black peppercorns
2 spring onions (scallions) or 1/2 onion, roughly chopped
1 tablespoon salt
4 skinless chicken breast fillets (200 g/7 oz each)
8 kipfler potatoes
12 asparagus spears
1 head of witlof (chicory/Belgian endive)

dressing

1 tablespoon finely chopped fresh chives
3 tablespoons extra virgin olive oil
2 tablespoons lemon juice
sea salt
freshly ground black pepper

Put the parsley, peppercorns, spring onion and salt into a large saucepan filled with cold water and bring to the boil. Add the chicken breasts, turn off the heat, put the lid on and leave the chicken to poach for 2 hours.

To make the dressing, stir the chives, oil, lemon juice and salt and pepper together in a bowl.

Bring a large saucepan of water to the boil and cook the potatoes for 15 minutes, or until tender. Drain and peel. Cut in slices and toss two-thirds of the dressing through. Keep warm. Blanch the asparagus in boiling water for 3 minutes, then refresh it in cold water.

Slice the chicken breasts on the diagonal. Divide the witlof leaves, potato and asparagus among four plates, top with slices of chicken and drizzle some dressing over the top. Serves 4

grilled tuna with green olive relish

2 tablespoons extra virgin olive oil
4 tuna steaks, about 150 g (5^1/$_2$ oz) each
sea salt
freshly ground black pepper

to serve
25 g (1 oz) baby English spinach leaves
green olive relish (below)
4 lemon cheeks (optional)

Brush the olive oil over the tuna steaks and season liberally with salt and pepper. Heat a large non-stick frying pan over a high heat, add the tuna and cook for 2 minutes each side. Remove from the pan and slice each steak into smaller pieces. Arrange on serving plates and serve with spinach leaves and relish. Serve with lemon cheeks if you wish. Serves 4

green olive relish

80 ml (1/3 cup) extra virgin olive oil
200 g (7 oz) green olives, pitted and sliced
2 celery stalks, finely diced
1 tablespoon red wine vinegar
2 garlic cloves, finely minced
1 fresh red chilli, seeded and finely diced
grated zest from 1 lemon
freshly ground black pepper
3 tablespoons roughly chopped fresh flat-leaf (Italian) parsley
sea salt (optional)

Stir all the relish ingredients together in a bowl until combined. Taste for seasoning and add a little sea salt, to taste, if desired.

ginger and prawn dumpling soup

1 kg (2 lb 4 oz) chicken bones
2 carrots, chopped
2 celery stalks, chopped
2 onions, chopped
a few fresh parsley stalks
6 peppercorns
500 g (1 lb 2 oz) raw medium prawns, peeled, deveined and chopped
2 tablespoons chopped fresh coriander (cilantro)
1 tablespoon oyster sauce
1 teaspoon grated ginger
1 teaspoon sesame oil
1/2 teaspoon salt
24 wonton skins

to serve
155 g (1 cup) fresh peas
a handful of baby spinach leaves

Put the chicken bones, carrot, celery, onion, parsley stalks and peppercorns in a stockpot with 4 litres (16 cups) of cold water and bring to the boil. Reduce the heat to low and simmer, uncovered, for 2 to 3 hours. Skim off any scum that rises to the surface. Strain the stock through a fine sieve.

To make the dumplings, mix the chopped prawns, coriander, oyster sauce, ginger, sesame oil and salt together in a bowl. Taking one wonton skin at a time, put a teaspoon of the filling in the middle, run a wet finger around the edge of the skin and then fold it in half to form a triangle. Seal the edges, then bring the two outside corners of the triangle together and pinch them so they stick — the dumplings will look sort of like tortellini.

Heat 1.5 litres (6 cups) of the strained stock in a saucepan until it boils, add the dumplings and the peas and cook them for a minute or two or until the dumplings float to the surface.

Divide the spinach leaves among four bowls and add some dumplings and peas to each. Pour a little of the stock over the top. Serves 4

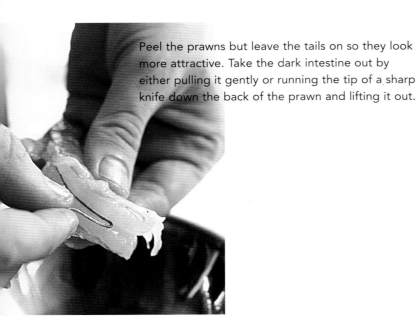

Peel the prawns but leave the tails on so they look more attractive. Take the dark intestine out by either pulling it gently or running the tip of a sharp knife down the back of the prawn and lifting it out.

prawn and avocado salad

2 limes, peeled and cut into quarters
sea salt
freshly ground black pepper
3 tablespoons fresh flat-leaf (Italian) parsley leaves
60 ml (1/4 cup) extra virgin olive oil
2 French shallots, finely sliced
2 tablespoons olive oil
20 raw medium prawns, peeled and deveined, tails left on
1 butter lettuce, washed, dried and shredded
2 avocados, each cut into eight pieces

Put seven lime quarters, the sea salt, pepper, parsley, olive oil and French shallots in a bowl and stir to combine. Squeeze the juice from the remaining lime quarter into the bowl.

Heat the olive oil in a frying pan, add the prawns and season with sea salt and pepper. Cook the prawns for about a minute on each side, or until they are nearly cooked — they will keep cooking for a short while after you take them off the heat.

Arrange some lettuce, avocado and prawns in four serving bowls or on plates. Drizzle a little dressing over each salad and serve. Serves 4

chicken salad with grapefruit and pistachios

4 skinless chicken breast fillets (200 g/7 oz each)
80 ml (^{1}/3 cup) extra virgin olive oil
1 lemon, sliced
freshly ground black pepper
sea salt
10 g (^{1}/2 cup) fresh flat-leaf (Italian) parsley leaves
10 g (^{1}/4 cup) fresh mint leaves
65 g (^{1}/4 cup) pistachios, roughly chopped
½ red onion, finely sliced
2 grapefruit, segmented

to serve
yoghurt dressing (below)

Slice each chicken breast into three escalopes. Put the chicken escalopes on a chopping board, put a freezer bag over them and pound them with a mallet or rolling pin until they are about 5 mm (^{1}/4 inch) thick.

Place the chicken escalopes in a flat ceramic dish and pour 60 ml (^{1}/4 cup) of the olive oil over them. Distribute the lemon and pepper over the chicken, cover and marinate in the fridge for 30 minutes.

Heat a large frying pan over a high heat for 2 minutes. Remove the chicken from the marinade and sprinkle it with sea salt. Cook in the pan for 1 minute each side or until cooked through and golden.

Toss the herbs with the pistachios, onion, grapefruit and remaining olive oil, then season well. Divide this among four plates and top each with three pieces of chicken. Serve with dressing on the side. Serves 4

yoghurt dressing

250 ml (1 cup) plain yoghurt
2 tablespoons olive oil
1 tablespoon lemon juice
salt
freshly ground black pepper

Stir all the dressing ingredients together in a small bowl.

I've used spaghettini in this recipe but you could use any type of long thin pasta such as linguine or spaghetti.

spaghettini with lemon, prosciutto and chilli

60 ml (1/4 cup) lemon juice
60 ml (1/4 cup) extra virgin olive oil
2 small fresh red chillies, seeded and finely chopped
12 slices prosciutto, cut into thin strips
1 tablespoon grated lemon zest
250 g (1 bunch) rocket (arugula) leaves, shredded
400 g (14 oz) good-quality dried thin spaghettini

Whisk the lemon juice, olive oil, chilli and some salt and pepper in a bowl to blend.

Put the prosciutto, lemon zest and the rocket leaves in a bowl and toss to combine.

Bring a large saucepan of salted water to the boil. Add the spaghettini and cook until *al dente*. Drain and add to the prosciutto and rocket. Pour the dressing over and toss to combine.

Transfer to a large serving dish or divide among four bowls. Remember, with simple recipes such as this one, you can throw in any of your favourite ingredients. Serves 4

crispy potato cake with a greek salad

750 g (1 lb 10 oz) all-purpose potatoes such as desiree
1 small onion
4 spring onions (scallions), finely sliced
2 eggs, lightly beaten
2 teaspoons plain (all-purpose) flour
15 g ($^1/_2$ cup) roughly chopped fresh flat-leaf (Italian) parsley
sea salt
freshly ground black pepper
1 tablespoon olive oil
Greek salad (below)

Grate the peeled potatoes and onion. This can be done in the food processor if you wish. Wrap them in a tea towel and squeeze out the excess moisture.

Put the potato, onion, spring onion, eggs, flour, parsley, salt and pepper into a bowl and stir to combine. Preheat the grill to its highest setting. Heat a 22 cm (9 inch) non-stick, ovenproof frying pan over a medium heat and add the olive oil. When the oil is hot, add the potato mixture and spread it out so that it covers the base of the pan. Cover and cook for about 10 minutes, shaking the pan frequently to stop the potato sticking. Heat under the grill for 6 to 7 minutes, until the potato cake is fully cooked and well browned. Turn out onto a serving platter, sprinkle with extra salt and pepper and cut into wedges. Serve with the Greek salad. Serves 4 to 6

greek salad

4 vine-ripened tomatoes, cut into wedges or chunks
2 Lebanese cucumbers, half-peeled in stripes, and cut into slices
1 green capsicum (pepper), sliced
$^1/_2$ red onion, finely sliced
2 tablespoons extra virgin olive oil
1 teaspoon red wine vinegar
16 Kalamata olives
12 fresh mint leaves
3 tablespoons fresh flat-leaf (Italian) parsley leaves
freshly ground black pepper
150 g (5$^1/_2$ oz) feta

Put the tomatoes, cucumber chunks, capsicum, onion and olive oil in a bowl. Toss to combine and set aside for 10 minutes. Add the vinegar, olives, mint, parsley and pepper and mix well. Transfer to a serving bowl and crumble the feta over the top.

Although I've used arborio rice here, you can use other risotto rices such as vialone nano or carnaroli.

crab and asparagus risotto

1.5 litres (6 cups) chicken or fish stock
1 tablespoon extra virgin olive oil
1 small onion, finely diced
1 teaspoon sea salt, plus extra, to taste
50 g ($1^3/4$ oz) butter
340 g ($1^1/2$ cups) arborio rice
8 asparagus spears, finely sliced on the diagonal
250 g (9 oz) fresh crab meat
grated zest from 1 lemon
60 ml ($1/4$ cup) lemon juice
salt
freshly ground black pepper
fresh chervil sprigs, for garnishing

Pour the stock into a saucepan and bring to the boil. Reduce the heat and keep at simmering point.

Place a large heavy-based saucepan over a medium heat and add the oil, onion, salt and half the butter. Stir until the onion is translucent. Add the rice and stir for 1 to 2 minutes, until the rice is well coated. Add a cupful of stock at a time, stirring constantly and being sure that each addition of stock is absorbed before you add more.

Continue adding stock for about 25 minutes. Add the asparagus and continue to add the remaining stock for about another 2 minutes, or until the rice is *al dente* and creamy. Remove the saucepan from the heat, stir in the remaining butter, the crab meat, lemon zest and juice, and salt and pepper, to taste. Cover the saucepan and leave to sit for 3 minutes to allow the flavours to develop. Stir and divide among four bowls. Top with chervil sprigs. Serves 4

honey-roasted duck breast with orange salad

2 tablespoons honey
2 tablespoons soy sauce
4 duck breast fillets, skin on
2 oranges
1 radicchio
30 g (1 bunch) fresh chives, cut into short lengths

dressing
2 tablespoons soy sauce
1 tablespoon balsamic vinegar
1 teaspoon sesame oil
2 teaspoons caster (superfine) sugar

Stir the honey and soy sauce together in a large bowl. Add the duck breasts and toss well. Cover and marinate in the fridge for at least 30 minutes.

Stir all the dressing ingredients together in a bowl until the sugar has dissolved.

Cut a slice from each end of the oranges and stand upright on a chopping board. With a sharp knife, cut away the peel, working from top to bottom, and removing as much of the white pith and peel as possible. Cut the orange segments out of their membranes.

Preheat the oven to 220°C (425°F/Gas 7). Heat an ovenproof frying pan over a medium to high heat for 1 minute. Cook the duck breasts with the skin side down for 3 minutes. Turn them over, then put the pan in the oven for 12 minutes. Remove from the oven, cover with foil and allow to rest for 5 minutes.

Slice each duck breast on the diagonal into thin slices. Arrange with the radicchio, orange slices and chives in four serving bowls or on plates. Spoon the dressing over the top. Serves 4

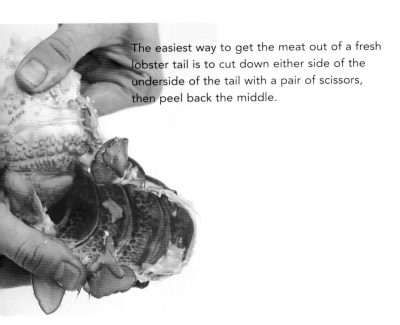

The easiest way to get the meat out of a fresh lobster tail is to cut down either side of the underside of the tail with a pair of scissors, then peel back the middle.

lobster sandwich

4 good-quality long white bread rolls
butter, softened
800 g (1 lb 12 oz) lobster, cooked and sliced (prawns are also delicious)
1 Lebanese cucumber, peeled and finely sliced

chive mayonnaise

125 g (1/2 cup) mayonnaise
2 tablespoons lemon juice
2 tablespoons chopped fresh chives
1/2 teaspoon Tabasco sauce
sea salt
freshly ground black pepper

Cut the bread rolls in half lengthways, leaving them attached along one side. Spread both halves with a little butter.

To make the chive mayonnaise, mix the mayonnaise with the remaining ingredients and season well with salt and pepper. Spread a layer over the bottom half of each roll and then top with alternating pieces of lobster and cucumber. Serves 4

You can use good-quality canned tuna
for this recipe. It is always an excellent standby to
have in the pantry.

warm pasta salad with tuna confit

500 ml (2 cups) olive oil
6 garlic cloves, crushed with the side of a knife
2 teaspoons black peppercorns
500 g (1 lb 2 oz) tuna steaks
200 g (7 oz) green beans
1 tablespoon red wine vinegar
sea salt
freshly ground black pepper
1 fresh red chilli, seeded and finely chopped
3 ripe tomatoes, cut into thin wedges, seeds removed
finely grated zest from 1 lemon
90 g ($^1/_2$ cup) small black olives, pitted and halved
$^1/_2$ small red onion, finely sliced into wedges
50 g ($^3/_4$ cup) roughly shredded fresh flat-leaf (Italian) parsley
400 g (14 oz) good-quality penne

Mix the oil, garlic and peppercorns in a large bowl, add the tuna, cover and marinate in the fridge
for 1 hour. Heat the tuna in the oil in a deep frying pan over medium heat until the oil is hot.
Reduce the heat and cook for 10 minutes. Remove the tuna from the oil, then allow the oil to cool.
Put the tuna back into the cooled oil, then cover and refrigerate until required (this tuna will store
in the fridge for up to four days).

Blanch the beans in boiling water for 2 minutes, then refresh in cold water. Flake the tuna into
large pieces. In a large bowl, stir 3 tablespoons of the tuna oil together with the vinegar, salt,
pepper, chopped chilli, tomato wedges, lemon zest, beans, tuna, olives, onion and parsley. Set
aside for 30 minutes for the flavours to develop.

Cook the penne in a large saucepan of rapidly boiling salted water until *al dente*. Drain well, then
toss the hot pasta with the tomato and tuna mixture. Stir well and serve. Serves 4

zucchini fritters with yoghurt sauce

500 g (1 lb 2 oz) zucchini (courgettes), grated
1/2 teaspoon sea salt
8 spring onions (scallions), chopped
125 g (41/2 oz) feta, crumbled
35 g (1/2 cup) chopped fresh flat-leaf (Italian) parsley
15 g (1/4 cup) chopped fresh mint
2 eggs, lightly beaten
60 g (1/2 cup) plain (all-purpose) flour
sea salt, extra, to taste
freshly ground black pepper
60 ml (1/4 cup) olive oil, for shallow-frying

to serve
yoghurt sauce (below)
lime wedges

Put the zucchini in a colander, sprinkle with the sea salt, toss lightly and set aside for 30 minutes. Squeeze out the excess liquid from the zucchini and pat dry with paper towels.

Put the zucchini, spring onion, feta, parsley, mint and eggs in a bowl and stir lightly to combine. Stir in the flour, salt and pepper.

Heat the oil in a non-stick frying pan over a medium to high heat. Drop tablespoons of batter into the hot oil, flattening gently with the back of a spoon. Cook for 2 minutes on each side, or until golden brown. Drain on paper towels and serve with yoghurt sauce and lime wedges. These fritters would also work really well with the Greek salad on page 59. Makes 18

yoghurt sauce

1 garlic clove, finely minced
1 tablespoon extra virgin olive oil
125 g (1/2 cup) plain yoghurt
2 tablespoons lemon juice
sea salt
freshly ground black pepper

Put all the ingredients in a bowl and stir to combine.

prawn and rice vermicelli salad

250 g (9 oz) rice vermicelli
125 ml (1/2 cup) soy sauce
60 ml (1/4 cup) rice vinegar
3 teaspoons oil mixed with 1 finely sliced chilli
11/2 tablespoons sugar
11/2 tablespoons peanut oil
3 cm x 4 cm (11/4 x 11/2 inch) piece of ginger, finely julienned
12 cooked prawns, shelled and deveined, and sliced in half lengthways
2 Lebanese cucumbers, julienned
4 spring onions (scallions), finely sliced on the diagonal

to serve
15 g (1/4 cup) fresh coriander (cilantro) sprigs
5 g (1/4 cup) fresh mint sprigs
lime wedges

Put the rice vermicelli in a bowl and pour in enough boiling water to cover. Soak for
6 to 7 minutes, then drain and refresh under cold water before draining thoroughly.

Stir the soy sauce, rice vinegar, chilli oil, sugar, peanut oil and ginger together in a large
bowl until the sugar is dissolved. Add the noodles, prawns, cucumber and spring onion and
stir carefully to combine.

Divide among four plates and top with coriander and mint. Serve with lime wedges. Serves 4

Sometimes I find store-bought olives a little too salty. Just soak them in water for an hour, drain and pour extra virgin olive oil over them. You could also add peppercorns, chillies, garlic cloves etc. for your own marinated olives.

spicy roast pumpkin, feta and olive salad

3 tablespoons olive oil
$1/2$ teaspoon ground cumin
$1/2$ teaspoon cayenne pepper
sea salt
freshly ground black pepper
800 g (1 lb 12 oz) pumpkin, cut into 2 cm ($3/4$ inch) cubes
100 g ($3^{1}/2$ oz) baby English spinach leaves
150 g ($5^{1}/2$ oz) marinated feta, drained and crumbled
20 Kalamata olives, pitted

dressing
1 tablespoon red wine vinegar
60 ml ($1/4$ cup) extra virgin olive oil
1 French shallot, finely sliced (optional)

Preheat the oven to 220°C (425°F/Gas 7). Place the olive oil, cumin, cayenne pepper, salt and pepper in a bowl and stir to combine. Add the pumpkin and stir to coat. Transfer to a roasting tin and bake for 30 minutes, or until the pumpkin is tender and slightly caramelized.

Whisk all the dressing ingredients together in a bowl until combined.

Divide the spinach leaves among four serving plates and scatter pumpkin, feta and olives over the top. Drizzle each salad with dressing. Serves 4

poached chicken and soba noodle salad with soy dressing

250 g (9 oz) soba noodles
soy dressing (below)
1 tablespoon black peppercorns
3 thick slices of ginger
2 spring onions (scallions), roughly chopped
2 tablespoons sea salt
4 skinless, free-range chicken breast fillets (200 g/7 oz each)
100 g (3^1/2 oz) snow pea (mangetout) sprouts
6 radishes, finely sliced

Bring a saucepan of water to the boil, add the noodles and cook for 3 minutes, or until *al dente*. Drain the noodles and rinse with cold water to cool them. Toss half the soy dressing through.

Put the peppercorns, ginger, spring onion and salt in a medium to large saucepan, fill with cold water and bring to the boil over a high heat. Add the chicken breasts and stir. Turn off the heat, cover with a tight-fitting lid and leave for 1 hour before cutting into slices.

Divide the noodles among four plates and spoon the remaining dressing over the top. Top with snow pea sprouts, sliced radish and the sliced poached chicken. Serves 4

soy dressing

60 ml (^{1}/4 cup) light or Japanese soy sauce
60 ml (^{1}/4 cup) mirin
2 tablespoons seasoned rice wine vinegar
1 garlic clove, finely chopped

Stir all the dressing ingredients together in a bowl until combined.

I love good tomatoes — and this salad makes great use of them — but make sure they are really ripe and that your basil is perfectly fresh.

tomato and olive salad with grilled herbed ricotta

750 g (3 cups) ricotta
4 tablespoons olive oil
sea salt
freshly ground black pepper
roughly chopped fresh sage, thyme and oregano
125 ml (1/2 cup) extra virgin olive oil
6 vine-ripened tomatoes
30 g (1 cup) fresh basil leaves
24 Niçoise olives
1 tablespoon balsamic vinegar

Distribute the ricotta and oil among six 125 ml (1/2 cup) ramekins. Sprinkle with salt and pepper, then scatter some sage, thyme and oregano over the top and drizzle with a little of the extra virgin olive oil. Grill under a high heat until bubbling.

Cut each tomato vertically into five slices, keeping the shape of the tomato intact.

Arrange the tomatoes on a platter, then top with the basil leaves and olives. Drizzle with the remaining olive oil and sprinkle with the balsamic vinegar. Season with salt and pepper, then allow to rest for 5 minutes so the flavours can develop before serving. Serve with the ricotta and some crusty bread. Serves 6

crispy-skinned salmon with fresh noodle salad and soy dressing

400 g (14 oz) fresh coriander (cilantro) egg noodles or other fresh egg noodles
4 salmon fillets, 2.5 cm (1 inch) thick, skin on
2 tablespoons oil
sea salt
freshly ground black pepper
1 cucumber, finely julienned
110 g (1 cup) finely julienned daikon radish
2 spring onions (scallions), finely sliced on the diagonal
soy dressing (below)

to serve
lime wedges

Bring a large saucepan of water to the boil over a high heat, add the noodles and blanch for 1 minute. Refresh under cold water.

Heat a frying pan over a high heat for 2 minutes. Brush the salmon fillets with oil and season liberally with salt and pepper. Cook the salmon with the skin side down for 2 minutes, then turn over and cook for another 2 minutes. Remove from the pan and allow to rest for 2 minutes. The salmon should be quite rare and the skin crispy.

To assemble the salad, divide the noodles among four plates. Arrange the cucumber and daikon over the noodles and sprinkle with spring onion. Put a salmon fillet on each plate and drizzle with soy dressing. Serve with lime wedges. Serves 4

soy dressing

2 teaspoons sesame oil
125 ml (1/2 cup) soy sauce
11/2 tablespoons balsamic vinegar
2 tablespoons caster (superfine) sugar
60 ml (1/4 cup) lime juice
2 fresh red chillies, finely chopped (optional)

Stir all the dressing ingredients together in a bowl until the sugar is dissolved.

afternoon tea

afternoon tea

'Afternoon tea is a good time to entertain, especially if you have small children who need to be at home in bed in the early evening. It's not a big entertaining call. It can be as simple as buying a cake but my scone recipe is so easy there's really no excuse for not cooking something as delicious as these yourself. It's not routinely done these days, so it's appreciated even more. There's also nothing like a plate of tasty chicken sandwiches and a pot of tea. Even with such simple food, afternoon teas feel luxurious. They're a celebration of the home-made in an era of mass-production and they're special because they indicate that you're giving time to people you care about. Many of the things I serve for afternoon tea are classics, and they are classics simply because they're good. I might modernize them and lighten them up, but they remain essentially unchanged. There's something very honest about baking at home.'

mandarin and almond cake

3 mandarins
250 g (1 cup) caster (superfine) sugar
6 eggs
230 g (2 cups) ground almonds

to serve
60 g (1/4 cup) caster (superfine) sugar
zest of 2 oranges
whipped cream

Put the mandarins in a medium saucepan and cover with water. Bring to the boil and simmer for 2 hours, adding water when necessary to keep the mandarins covered at all times.

Preheat the oven to 160°C (315°F/Gas 2–3). Drain the mandarins and cool to room temperature. Once cooled, split them open with your hands and remove any seeds. Purée the mandarins, including the skins, in a food processor.

Whisk the sugar and eggs together in a large bowl until combined. Add the ground almonds and mandarin purée and stir thoroughly.

Pour the mixture into a well-greased 24 cm (9 inch) springform cake tin and bake for 1 hour 10 minutes, or until the cake looks set in the middle, springs back when touched and comes away from the edges. Remove from the oven and allow to cool in the tin.

While the cake is cooling, put the sugar in a saucepan with 60 ml (1/4 cup) of water over a low heat and stir until the sugar dissolves. Add the orange zest and boil the mixture until it just starts to caramelize. Lift the zest out with a fork and cool it on a plate.

Serve the cake with lightly whipped cream and caramelized citrus zest. Serves 10 to 12

heart shortbread kisses

40 g (¹/3 cup) icing (confectioners') sugar, sifted
250 g (9 oz) unsalted butter, softened
1 teaspoon vanilla extract
60 g (¹/2 cup) cornflour (cornstarch)
185 g (1¹/2 cups) plain (all-purpose) flour
a pinch of salt
80 g (¹/4 cup) raspberry jam
icing (confectioners') sugar for dusting

Beat the sugar and butter together in a bowl until just combined. Add the vanilla extract, sifted flours and salt and mix until a dough forms. Mould into a log 6 cm (2¹/2 inches) in diameter, wrap in plastic wrap and refrigerate for 30 minutes.

Preheat the oven to 180°C (350°F/Gas 4). Remove the dough from the fridge and cut into 7 mm (³/8 inch) slices, then cut shapes with a 5 cm (2 inch) heart biscuit cutter. Reroll the excess dough and repeat the process until all the dough is used up.

Place the hearts on greased and lined baking trays and bake for 15 to 20 minutes, until golden brown. Transfer the shortbread biscuits to wire racks and leave to cool completely. Spread half of the biscuits with jam, top with the remaining biscuits and sprinkle with icing sugar.
Makes 15 double shortbread kisses.

plum and vanilla cake

topping
90 g (^{3}/4 cup) plain (all-purpose) flour
100 g (3^1/2 oz) unsalted butter, chopped into small pieces
90 g (^{1}/3 cup) caster (superfine) sugar

cake
180 g (6 oz) unsalted butter, softened
250 g (1 cup) caster (superfine) sugar
3 eggs, lightly beaten
1 teaspoon vanilla extract
185 g (1^1/2 cups) plain (all-purpose) flour
2 teaspoons baking powder
500 g (1 lb 2 oz) fresh plums, halved and seeded,
    or 825 g (1 lb 13 oz) canned plums, seeded

Preheat the oven to 180°C (350°F/Gas 4). To make the topping, place the flour, butter and sugar in a bowl and rub with your fingertips until crumbly (this can be done in a food processor if you prefer).

To make the cake, cream the butter and sugar together in a bowl until light and fluffy. Add the eggs, one at a time, beating well after each addition. Mix in the vanilla extract. Sift the flour and baking powder into the bowl and fold into the mixture. Spread into a 24 cm (9 inch) greased or non-stick springform cake tin. Top with halved plums with the cut side up. Sprinkle with the topping and bake for 1 hour, or until a skewer inserted into the centre of the cake comes out clean.

Remove from the oven and allow to cool in the tin for 10 minutes. Delicious served with pouring cream. Serves 10 to 12

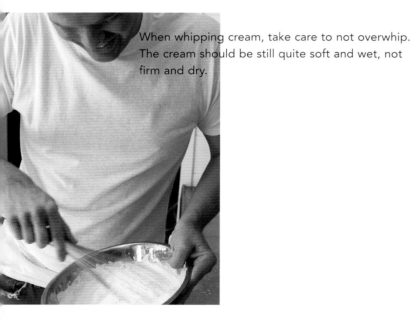

When whipping cream, take care to not overwhip. The cream should be still quite soft and wet, not firm and dry.

simple scones

1 tablespoon icing (confectioners') sugar
310 g (2^1/2 cups) plain (all-purpose) flour
1^1/2 tablespoons baking powder
a pinch of salt
250 ml (1 cup) milk
30 g (1 oz) butter, melted

to serve
jam
whipped cream

Preheat the oven to 220°C (425°F/Gas 7). Sift the icing sugar, flour, baking powder and salt into a bowl. Add the milk and butter and stir to combine with a knife. Knead quickly and lightly until smooth and then press out onto a floured surface.

Use a glass to cut out rounds roughly 5 cm (2 inches) in diameter and 3 cm (1^1/4 inches) deep and place them close together on a greased baking tray. Gather the scraps together, lightly knead again, then cut out more rounds. Cook for 8 to 10 minutes, until puffed and golden. Serve with jam and lightly whipped cream. Makes 8

coconut blackberry slice

base
125 g (4¹/2 oz) unsalted butter
60 g (¹/4 cup) caster (superfine) sugar
1 egg
1 teaspoon vanilla extract
185 g (1¹/2 cups) plain (all-purpose) flour
1 teaspoon baking powder
60 ml (¹/4 cup) milk

filling
175 g (¹/2 cup) blackberry jam
250 g (1 cup) blackberries

topping
100 g (3¹/2 oz) unsalted butter
5 tablespoons caster (superfine) sugar
2 eggs
225 g (2¹/2 cups) desiccated coconut
60 g (¹/2 cup) plain (all-purpose) flour

Preheat the oven to 180°C (350°F/Gas 4). To make the base, cream the butter and sugar in a bowl until light and fluffy. Add the egg and vanilla extract and stir to combine. Sift the flour and baking powder into the bowl and stir in with the milk. Flour your hands and press the base evenly into a greased and lined 30 x 20 cm (12 x 8 inch) baking tin. Spread the base evenly with jam and sprinkle with blackberries.

To make the topping, cream the butter and sugar in a bowl until light and fluffy. Add the egg and beat until combined. Stir in the coconut and 1 tablespoon sifted flour, then stir in the remaining flour. Spread the topping evenly over the blackberries.

Bake the slice for 30 minutes, or until golden. Cover with foil and cook for another 5 minutes. Remove from the oven and allow to cool in the tin for 10 minutes. Cut into rectangles. Makes 20

pear and vanilla cake with custard

80 g (3 oz) unsalted butter
185 g (3/4 cup) caster (superfine) sugar
1 egg
1 teaspoon vanilla extract
grated zest from 1 lemon
185 ml (3/4 cup) cream
165 g (1 1/3 cups) plain (all-purpose) flour
2 teaspoons baking powder
a pinch of salt
4 pears
20 g (3/4 oz) unsalted butter, melted
60 g (1/4 cup) raw sugar
custard (below)

Preheat the oven to 180°C (350°F/Gas 4). Cream the butter and sugar together in a bowl until light and fluffy. Add the egg, vanilla and lemon zest and beat for another minute. Add the cream and mix until smooth. Sift in the flour, baking powder and salt and beat until smooth. Pour into a 24 cm (9 inch) non-stick springform cake tin and smooth the surface.

Peel and core the pears, cut into 3 mm (1/8 inch) slices and arrange on the batter in two concentric circles. Brush the pears with melted butter, then sprinkle with the raw sugar. Bake for 50 minutes to 1 hour, or until a skewer comes out clean and the pears on top are lightly browned. Remove the side from the cake tin and slide the cake onto a plate. Cool slightly before slicing. Serve with custard. Serves 6 to 8

custard

250 ml (1 cup) milk
185 ml (3/4 cup) cream
1 teaspoon vanilla extract
4 egg yolks
1 egg
2 tablespoons caster (superfine) sugar

Gently heat the milk, cream and vanilla in a small saucepan. Whisk the egg yolks, egg and sugar together in a small bowl, then whisk in the milk mixture until smooth. Transfer to a small saucepan and stir over a low heat for 10 minutes, or until the mixture is thick enough to coat the back of a spoon. Remove from the heat, cover and keep warm.

white chocolate cheesecake

100 g (3^1/$_2$ oz) plain sweet biscuits
50 g (1^3/$_4$ oz) butter, melted
250 ml (1 cup) cream
250 g (9 oz) cream cheese
250 g (9 oz) mascarpone cheese
125 g (^{1}/$_2$ cup) caster (superfine) sugar
500 g (1 lb 2 oz) white chocolate, melted

to serve
passionfruit pulp

Process the biscuits in a food processor until they look like breadcrumbs. Add the melted butter, process briefly, then tip the mixture into a 20 cm (8 inch) springform tin lined with a disc of baking paper. Press the biscuit mixture firmly into the base of the tin, then put the tin in the fridge until you need it.

Using electric beaters, whisk the cream, cream cheese, mascarpone, sugar and chocolate together until smooth. Pour this mixture onto the biscuit base and put the cheesecake back into the fridge for at least 3 hours or overnight. Serve drizzled with passionfruit pulp and cut into wedges. Serves 8

buttermilk cake with raspberry syrup

125 g (4 1/2 oz) unsalted butter, softened
250 g (1 cup) caster (superfine) sugar
2 eggs
250 ml (1 cup) buttermilk
1 teaspoon vanilla extract
250 g (2 cups) plain (all-purpose) flour
2 teaspoons baking powder
a pinch of salt
raspberry syrup (below)

to serve
whipped cream

Preheat the oven to 180°C (350°F/Gas 4). Using electric beaters, cream the butter and sugar until pale and fluffy. Add the eggs, one at a time, beating well after each addition. With the mixer at low speed, beat in the buttermilk and the vanilla extract until just combined. Sift in the flour, baking powder and salt in two batches, mixing well after each addition.

Spoon the mixture into a greased and lined 20 cm (8 inch) cake tin and smooth the top. Bake for 45 to 50 minutes, or until a skewer comes out clean. Leave to cool in the tin for 10 minutes, then transfer to a plate and pour syrup over the top.

Place slices of cake on serving plates with some lightly whipped cream and raspberries.
Serves 8 to 10

raspberry syrup

60 g (1/2 cup) sugar
2 tablespoons lemon juice
220 g (8 oz) raspberries, plus a few for serving

Stir the sugar, lemon juice and 1/4 cup (60 ml) water in a saucepan over a medium to high heat until the sugar dissolves. Cook for 2 to 3 minutes, then add the raspberries and lightly crush with the back of a spoon. Cook for another 3 minutes, then remove from the heat and purèe in a blender.

I like to serve lime slice with mint tea. Put some fresh mint leaves in a glass and top up with boiling water. Add some honey if you have a sweet tooth.

lime slice

base
200 g (7 oz) unsalted butter, softened and chopped
250 g (2 cups) plain (all-purpose) flour
30 g (1/4 cup) icing (confectioners') sugar
1 egg, lightly beaten

filling
6 eggs
375 g (1 1/2 cups) caster (superfine) sugar
60 g (1/2 cup) plain (all-purpose) flour
125 ml (1/2 cup) lime juice
finely grated zest from 4 limes
icing (confectioners') sugar, for dusting

Grease and line the base and sides of a 23 cm (9 inch) square tin with baking paper. To make the base, mix the butter, flour, icing sugar and egg together in a food processor until a dough forms. Press the dough into the tin. Refrigerate the dough in the tin for 30 minutes. Preheat the oven to 180°C (350°F/Gas 4), then bake the base for 20 to 25 minutes, until pale golden.

While the base is cooking, make the filling. Whisk the eggs in a bowl, then add the sugar, flour, lime juice and zest, and whisk until combined.

Pour the filling onto the cooked base and bake for another 20 minutes, or until the filling is set and lightly golden on top. Remove from the oven and allow to cool in the tin.

Cut into pieces and dust with icing sugar. Makes 12

strawberry shortcakes

100 g (3^1/2 oz) cold unsalted butter, cut into small pieces
250 g (2 cups) plain (all-purpose) flour
60 g (^{1}/4 cup) caster (superfine) sugar
1 tablespoon baking powder
a pinch of salt
125 ml (^{1}/2 cup) cream
1 egg
1 egg yolk, extra
1 tablespoon cream, extra
450 g (3 cups) strawberries
90 g (^{1}/4 cup) honey
1 tablespoon lemon juice

to serve
double (thick) cream
icing (confectioners') sugar, for sprinkling

Preheat the oven to 200°C (400°F/Gas 6). Process the pieces of butter with the flour, sugar, baking powder and salt in a food processor until the mixture resembles coarse breadcrumbs. Transfer to a large bowl.

Mix the cream and egg in a small bowl until combined, then add to the flour and butter mixture and fold in with a knife until just combined. Turn out the dough onto a lightly floured surface and pat out to 2.5 cm (1 inch) thick. Cut out six rounds with a 7 cm (2^3/4 inch) cutter. Place on a baking tray lined with baking paper.

Mix the extra egg yolk and cream and brush on top of the dough rounds. Bake for 20 to 25 minutes, or until lightly golden. Cool on wire racks for 15 minutes.

While the shortcakes are cooking, slice the strawberries and put them in a bowl. Add the honey and lemon juice and stir to combine.

To serve, slice open each shortcake with a knife and place the bottom halves on a plate. Top each with cream and strawberries, then replace the tops of the shortcakes. Sprinkle with icing sugar. Makes 6

dinner

dinner

'The older I get the more simply I like to eat and the more I appreciate uncomplicated things. Depending on the mood I'm trying to create, anything goes. But, if I have time, I enjoy cooking a complicated dinner with the day spent shopping and cooking something challenging. I also love an appreciative audience when cooking — nothing satisfies me more than feeding hungry friends. I have a few golden rules that I have learnt over the years. Never have a glass of wine before the guests arrive or you will lose focus. Prepare everything you possibly can beforehand and, unless you are lucky enough to have a lovely open kitchen, try not to be cooking when they come. People love to be given jobs like setting the table and picking watercress, so don't be afraid to delegate — I never am! I find dessert is always appreciated as a treat, but it doesn't have to be rich or difficult to make. It can be as simple as vanilla ice cream with fresh berries, a block of chocolate broken up, or a bowl of cherries on ice. Remember, just keep it simple.'

To make ricotta toasts, spread some ricotta on slices of bread, drizzle with olive oil and grill.

spicy tomato and fennel soup

2 kg (4^1/$_2$ lb) vine-ripened tomatoes
6 garlic cloves, peeled
1 small carrot, diced
^{1}/$_2$ small fennel bulb, finely chopped
60 ml (^{1}/$_4$ cup) extra virgin olive oil
2 tablespoons sea salt
freshly ground black pepper

to serve
a handful of fresh basil leaves (optional)
extra virgin olive oil
ricotta toast (see above)

Preheat the oven to 200°C (400°F/Gas 6). Place the tomatoes, garlic, carrot and fennel in a roasting tin. Drizzle with olive oil and sprinkle with salt and pepper. Cover with foil and bake for 1^1/$_2$ hours. Uncover and bake for another 30 minutes, or until the vegetables are well cooked.

Transfer the vegetables to a food processor or blender and blend until combined. What you are looking for is a smoothish mixture with some texture. If you prefer a completely smooth consistency, you can pass the soup through a sieve, but I personally love it with a bit of texture.

Serve in soup bowls. Top each with basil leaves if you wish and a drizzle of extra virgin olive oil. Serve with ricotta toast. Serves 4

Using ground rice makes the fritters more crisp. You can make your own ground rice by grinding rice in the food processor.

corn fritters with sweet chilli sauce

90 g (1/2 cup) ground rice or plain (all-purpose) flour
60 g (1/2 cup) plain (all-purpose) flour
1/4 teaspoon baking powder
1/2 teaspoon salt
1 teaspoon ground coriander
1/2 teaspoon ground cumin
1 egg, lightly beaten
1 teaspoon lemon juice
350 g (2 cups) corn kernels, cut from 3 large corn cobs
4 spring onions (scallions), finely sliced
3 tablespoons chopped fresh coriander (cilantro)
60 ml (1/4 cup) oil

to serve
sweet chilli sauce (see page 128)

Sift the ground rice, flour, baking powder, salt, coriander and cumin into a bowl. Add the egg, lemon juice and 125 ml (1/2 cup) water and beat to a smooth batter. Add the corn, spring onion and chopped coriander and stir to combine.

Heat the oil in a large non-stick frying pan over a medium to high heat. When the oil is hot, add 2 tablespoons of mixture for each fritter and flatten with the back of a spoon. Cook for about 2 to 3 minutes, or until golden brown, then turn and cook the other side. Serve with the sweet chilli sauce. Garnish the sauce with coriander leaves if you like. Makes 24

individual lasagne with ricotta, zucchini and tomato

2 x 400 g (14 oz) cans chopped Roma (plum) tomatoes
1 garlic clove, crushed
2 tablespoons extra virgin olive oil
sea salt
freshly ground black pepper
a pinch of sugar
500 g (1 lb 2 oz) ricotta
40 g (1^1/$_2$ oz) freshly grated Parmesan
1 tablespoon fresh oregano leaves
375 g (13 oz) fresh lasagne sheets
2 zucchini (courgettes), finely sliced on the diagonal
fresh oregano leaves, for garnishing

Preheat the oven to 200°C (400°F/Gas 6). Cook the tomatoes in a medium saucepan over a medium to low heat for 20 minutes, or until slightly reduced. Add the garlic, olive oil, salt, pepper and sugar and cook for another minute. Remove from the heat.

Stir the ricotta, Parmesan, oregano and some salt and pepper together in a bowl.

Cut the lasagne sheets into sixteen 10 cm (4 inch) squares and cook them, a few at a time, in a large saucepan of boiling salted water until *al dente*. Transfer to a bowl filled with cold water and a few drops of olive oil. When the sheets are cool, drain and place on a tea towel.

Pour 185 ml (³/4 cup) of the tomato sauce into a large roasting tin and spread to cover the base. Place four lasagne squares on the tomato sauce, keeping them separate. Spoon one-third of the ricotta mixture evenly among the squares and top with one-third of the zucchini slices. Place a second square on top of each and repeat the process to give four layers, finishing with lasagne squares. Spoon 2 tablespoons sauce over each stack. Bake for about 25 minutes, until hot.

Serve with extra sauce and sprinkled with oregano leaves. Serves 4

To change the flavour of this soup, just use different types of mushrooms. Darker ones will give a richer flavour, whereas lighter ones will give a more delicate flavour.

mushroom soup

350 g (12 oz) button mushrooms
250 g (9 oz) potatoes, peeled and roughly chopped
25 g (1 oz) butter
2 tablespoons olive oil
2 garlic cloves, finely chopped
125 ml (^{1}/2 cup) dry white wine
2 teaspoons finely chopped fresh oregano
1.5 litres (6 cups) chicken stock or water

to serve
fresh parsley sprigs
4 tablespoons sour cream (optional)

Finely chop the mushrooms in a food processor using the pulse action. Remove and repeat the process with the potatoes.

Heat the butter and oil in a large saucepan over a medium heat. Add the mushrooms, garlic and a little salt and pepper, and cook for 10 minutes. Add the potato, wine, oregano and stock and bring to the boil over a high heat. Reduce the heat to low and simmer for 25 minutes. Let the soup cool slightly, then transfer 375 ml (1^1/2 cups) of the soup to a blender and chop until smooth. Return to the saucepan and stir well.

Ladle into serving bowls, top with a sprig of parsley and a tablespoon of sour cream if you wish.
Serves 4

garlic prawns

20 raw king prawns, peeled and deveined, tails left on
250 ml (1 cup) olive oil
5 garlic cloves, finely chopped
3 fresh small red chillies, split lengthways but intact at top
1 teaspoon sea salt
freshly ground black pepper
2 tablespoons chopped fresh flat-leaf (Italian) parsley

to serve
lemon wedges
crusty bread
green salad

Preheat the oven to 250°C (500°F/Gas 9). Cut a slit down the back of each prawn and place the prawns in an ovenproof dish that will hold them snugly in a single layer.

Heat the oil in a large ovenproof frying pan over a high heat. Add half the garlic and all the chillies and cook for 1 minute or until the garlic starts to change colour. Pour over the prawns, then sprinkle with the remaining garlic. Season with salt and pepper, cover with foil and bake for 10 minutes, or until the prawns are pink and cooked through. Don't overcook — remember that the prawns will continue cooking after being removed from the oven. Serve in a large bowl or divide among four serving dishes. Sprinkle with parsley and serve with lemon wedges, crusty bread and a green salad. Serves 4

poussin with spicy corn salad

4 poussin, rinsed and dried with paper towel
sea salt
freshly ground black pepper
1 lime
2 tablespoons olive oil

to serve
spicy corn salad (below)
3 tablespoons fresh coriander (cilantro) leaves (optional)

Preheat the oven to 220°C (425°F/Gas 7). Season the poussin liberally with salt and pepper inside and out. Thinly slice the lime and squeeze some of the juice over the skin of the poussin. Put some lime slices into each poussin cavity, then tie the legs together with kitchen string.

Place the poussin with their breast sides up in a roasting tin and drizzle with olive oil. Bake for 35 minutes, or until golden and cooked. Serve with spicy corn salad and coriander leaves.
Serves 4

spicy corn salad

350 g (2 cups) corn kernels, cut from 2 corn cobs
200 g (7 oz) green beans, trimmed and sliced diagonally into 1 cm (^{1}/2 inch) pieces
60 ml (^{1}/4 cup) extra virgin olive oil
80 ml (^{1}/3 cup) lime juice
1 green chilli, seeded and finely chopped (optional)
sea salt
freshly ground black pepper
^{1}/2 teaspoon cayenne pepper
^{1}/4 teaspoon ground cumin
^{1}/2 small red capsicum (pepper), finely diced
6 spring onions (scallions), diagonally sliced
7 g (^{1}/4 cup) chopped fresh coriander (cilantro)

Bring a saucepan of water to the boil over a high heat, add the corn kernels and green beans and cook for 30 seconds. Drain and refresh under cold running water.

Whisk the olive oil, lime juice, chilli, sea salt, pepper, cayenne pepper and cumin together in a large bowl to combine. Add the corn, beans and remaining ingredients and stir to combine. Allow to rest for 20 minutes so the flavours can develop. Stir again and serve.

spaghetti with spicy meatballs

80 ml (1/3 cup) milk
1 slice of bread, crust removed
500 g (1 lb 2 oz) beef mince, or pork and veal mince
1 small onion, finely chopped
2 tablespoons chopped fresh flat-leaf (Italian) parsley
1 teaspoon finely chopped fresh thyme
1 egg, lightly beaten
25 g (1/4 cup) freshly grated Parmesan
2 garlic cloves, finely minced
2 fresh red chillies, finely chopped
sea salt
freshly ground black pepper
60 ml (1/4 cup) olive oil
2 x 400 g (14 oz) cans chopped Roma (plum) tomatoes
50 g (1/2 cup) fresh basil leaves, shredded
500 g (1 lb 2 oz) spaghetti

to serve
a handful of fresh basil leaves
freshly grated Parmesan cheese

Put the milk and bread in a small saucepan and place over a low heat. When the bread has absorbed the milk, remove from the heat and mash with a fork. Allow to cool.

Combine the meat, onion, parsley, thyme, egg, Parmesan, garlic, half of the chilli, the bread mixture and lots of salt and pepper in a large bowl. Gently mix with your hands, then shape into small balls. I find wetting my hands makes this easier.

Heat the oil in a large frying pan over a medium heat and, when hot, add the meatballs. Brown the meatballs on all sides, turning carefully. Alternatively, you can toss the meatballs in oil in a roasting tin and bake them at 220°C (425°F/Gas 7) for 10 to 15 minutes. You may find this easier because the meatballs won't break up. Drain off any excess oil (if you've baked the meatballs, transfer them to a frying pan) and add the tomatoes, remaining chilli, basil and salt and pepper. Stir the meatballs carefully to coat with the tomatoes, then simmer for 20 minutes.

While the meatballs are cooking, bring a large saucepan of water to the boil over a high heat. Add the spaghetti and cook, according to the manufacturer's instructions, until *al dente*.

To serve, divide the drained spaghetti among four bowls and spoon over the meatballs and sauce. Sprinkle with extra basil leaves and serve with freshly grated Parmesan. Serves 4 to 6

Calasparra is a type of Spanish short-grain rice that
works very well in this recipe. You can, of course,
use other types of short-grain rice.

saffron rice with prawns

80 ml (1/3 cup) olive oil
300 g (10 1/2 oz) French shallots, sliced
sea salt
400 g (14 oz) can chopped Roma (plum) tomatoes
2 pinches of saffron
1 teaspoon sweet paprika
225 g (8 oz) jar of chopped pimentos
freshly ground black pepper
1.25 litres (5 cups) chicken stock
300 g (10 1/2 oz) green beans, sliced into 1 cm (1/2 inch) pieces
500 g (1 lb 2 oz) Spanish calasparra rice (or arborio)
24 raw king prawns, shelled and deveined, tails left on

to serve
lemon wedges
finely chopped fresh parsley

Heat a large saucepan over a medium to high heat and add half the olive oil. Add half the shallots and sprinkle liberally with sea salt. Cook for 5 minutes, stirring occasionally. Add the tomatoes, saffron, paprika, half the jar of pimentos, the pepper and stock and simmer for 20 minutes. Add the beans and cook for another 5 minutes.

When you add the beans, heat a large frying pan or paella pan over a medium to high heat and add the remaining oil. Add the remaining shallots and cook for 5 minutes, stirring occasionally. Add the rice and cook for another 2 minutes, stirring to coat all the grains with oil. Add the tomato mixture and the remaining pimentos and simmer over a low heat, stirring occasionally, for 15 minutes. Add the prawns, stir to combine, then cook, without stirring, for another 10 minutes, or until the prawns are pink. Serve with lemon wedges and parsley. Serves 6

glazed honey and soy chicken with sweet chilli sauce

125 ml (1/2 cup) soy sauce
2 tablespoons vegetable oil
2 tablespoons honey
2 tablespoons shaosing wine or dry sherry
1 garlic clove, finely crushed
1 tablespoon finely grated ginger
1 fresh red chilli, finely chopped
4 chicken Marylands (leg quarters), cut into 2 pieces between thigh and drumstick

to serve
cucumber slices
fresh coriander (cilantro) sprigs
lime or lemon wedges
steamed rice
sweet chilli sauce (below)

Preheat the oven to 180°C (350°F/Gas 4). Stir all the ingredients, except the chicken, together in a small bowl. Put the chicken in a bowl or flat dish, pour the marinade over and mix with your hands to coat. Cover and marinate in the fridge for at least 1 hour, or overnight.

Remove the chicken from the marinade and place, with the skin side up, in a roasting tin. Bake for 45 minutes, frequently turning the drumsticks over as they brown, and basting the chicken every 15 minutes with extra marinade. Use a cleaver to cut the chicken into pieces.

Serve with fresh cucumber, coriander sprigs, lime wedges and steamed rice, with sweet chilli sauce on the side. Serves 4

sweet chilli sauce

3 large fresh red chillies, finely chopped
250 ml (1 cup) rice vinegar
2 teaspoons salt
185 g (3/4 cup) sugar
1 large garlic clove, chopped

Combine all the ingredients in a small saucepan and stir over a low heat until the sugar dissolves. Bring to the boil, then cook for 5 minutes, or until the mixture thickens to a slightly syrupy consistency. Remove from the heat and allow to cool.

grilled lamb with a warm chickpea salad

2 tablespoons olive oil
1/2 teaspoon ground cumin
1/2 teaspoon cayenne pepper
12 French-trimmed lamb cutlets
1 small white onion, finely chopped
zest from 2 lemons
2 tablespoons chopped fresh flat-leaf (Italian) parsley
1 tablespoon chopped fresh mint
2 tablespoons lemon juice
sea salt
freshly ground black pepper

to serve
4 lemon wedges
warm chickpea salad (below)

Stir the olive oil, cumin and cayenne pepper together in a small bowl and brush the mixture over the cutlets.

Put the onion, lemon zest, parsley, mint, lemon juice, salt and pepper in a small bowl and stir well.

Heat a large frying pan over a high heat, then add the cutlets and cook for 2 minutes each side, remembering that you want the meat still pink. Remove from the pan and rest the meat on a large platter.

Before serving, spoon the onion and herb mixture over the cutlets. Serve with lemon wedges and the warm chickpea salad. Serves 4

warm chickpea salad

400 g (14 oz) can chickpeas, drained
1 celery stalk, finely sliced
65 g (1/2 cup) finely sliced fennel
1 garlic clove, crushed
2 tablespoons lemon juice
2 tablespoons extra virgin olive oil
sea salt
freshly ground black pepper
3 tablespoons fresh flat-leaf (Italian) parsley, torn

Bring a medium saucepan of water to the boil over a high heat, add the chickpeas, heat for 30 seconds, then drain and transfer to a bowl. Add the remaining ingredients and stir well.

lemon and parsley crusted fish with garlic mashed potatoes

80 g (1 cup) fresh breadcrumbs (I like brown but can be white)
1 garlic clove, roughly chopped
15 g (^{1}/2 cup) roughly chopped fresh flat-leaf (Italian) parsley
finely grated zest from 1 lemon
sea salt
freshly ground black pepper
2 tablespoons olive oil
4 thick (about 3 cm/1^1/4 inch) white fish fillets such as mahi mahi or blue-eye

to serve
50 g (1^3/4 oz) baby English spinach leaves
4 lemon wedges
garlic mashed potatoes (below)

Preheat the oven to 220°C (425°F/Gas 7). Place the breadcrumbs, garlic, parsley, lemon zest, salt, pepper, and half the olive oil in a food processor and pulse to just combine until you have pale green breadcrumbs.

Place the fish on a baking tray lined with baking paper and press some crumbs over the top of each piece of fish. Drizzle with the remaining olive oil and bake for 10 minutes, or until the crust is golden and the fish is just cooked.

Serve with baby spinach leaves, lemon wedges and garlic mashed potatoes. Serves 4

garlic mashed potatoes

800 g (1 lb 12 oz) potatoes, suitable for mashing, such as pontiac or desiree
250 ml (1 cup) milk
75 g (2^1/2 oz) butter
3 garlic cloves, bruised
1 teaspoon sea salt

Cut the potatoes into quarters and cook them in boiling water until tender. Remove from the heat, drain, then mash the potatoes in the saucepan.

Meanwhile, heat the milk, butter and garlic in a small saucepan over a medium heat until hot, making sure you don't let the mixture boil. Remove from the heat.

When the potatoes are nearly cooked, reheat the milk over a low heat, then remove and discard the garlic cloves. Mix the milk mixture into the potatoes with a wooden spoon until smooth. Season with salt, to taste.

In any recipe that uses coconut milk, I use low-fat
soy milk for guilt-free eating.

grilled chicken with spicy coconut sauce

4 chicken breast fillets, skin on (about 280 g/10 oz each)
2 tablespoons vegetable oil
sea salt
freshly ground black pepper
310 ml (1^1/4 cups) coconut milk or low-fat soy milk
75 g (^{1}/4 cup) laksa paste
400 g (14 oz) fresh egg noodles
200 g (7 oz) snow peas (mangetout), blanched and finely sliced diagonally

to serve
lime cheeks

Preheat the oven to 220°C (425°F/Gas 7). Put the chicken, oil, salt and pepper in a bowl and
toss to combine. Heat an ovenproof frying pan (large enough to hold the chicken fillets in one
layer) over a high heat. Place the chicken with the skin side down in the pan and sear for about
4 to 5 minutes until golden. Turn the chicken over and cook it for another minute to seal it. Put
the pan in the oven and cook the chicken for about 10 minutes, until the chicken feels firm to
touch. Remove from the oven, leave to rest for 5 minutes, then cut each fillet on the diagonal
into three pieces.

Meanwhile, stir the coconut milk and laksa paste in a small saucepan over a medium heat until
combined. Cook for 5 minutes, or until reduced slightly.

While the chicken and sauce are cooking, cook the noodles in boiling, salted water for
1 minute. Drain and divide among four shallow serving bowls. Top with finely sliced snow
peas and sliced chicken. Pour the sauce over. Serve with lime cheeks. Serves 4

pan-fried lemon veal with green beans

8 veal escalopes
1 teaspoon sea salt
freshly ground black pepper
300 g (10^1/$_2$ oz) baby green beans, trimmed
2 tablespoons extra virgin olive oil
4 tablespoons lemon juice
50 g (1^3/$_4$ oz) butter
2 tablespoons finely chopped fresh flat-leaf (Italian) parsley

to serve
4 lemon wedges

Season the veal with the sea salt and black pepper.

Steam the green beans in a steamer for 3 minutes. While the beans are cooking, heat the oil in a large frying pan over a medium to high heat. When the oil is hot, add the veal and cook for about 45 seconds on each side.

Reduce the frying pan heat to low and add the lemon juice, loosening the residue from the base of the pan. When the lemon juice boils, add the butter and mix until the butter melts and the sauce is slightly thickened. Pour over the veal and sprinkle with chopped parsley. Serve with the green beans and lemon wedges. Serves 4

veal cutlets with tomatoes, capers and polenta

4 large ripe tomatoes, each cut into eight wedges
1 tablespoon fresh oregano leaves
2 tablespoons capers, rinsed and squeezed dry
2 garlic cloves, sliced
1 red onion, cut into fine wedges
2 tablespoons olive oil
sea salt
freshly ground black pepper
4 veal cutlets

to serve
polenta (below)

Preheat the oven to 200°C (400°F/Gas 6). If you intend to serve these cutlets with polenta, start cooking your polenta now.

Put the tomatoes, oregano, capers, garlic, onion and olive oil in a small roasting tin (large enough to fit the veal cutlets) and toss together. Sprinkle with salt and pepper. Cover with foil and bake for 25 to 30 minutes. Remove the foil and bake for another 10 minutes.

While the tomatoes are cooking, brush the veal cutlets with oil and season liberally with salt and pepper. Heat a large frying pan over a high heat for 1 to 2 minutes, until very hot. Add the veal cutlets and cook for 1 minute on each side, or until the veal is sealed. Remove from the pan.

Place the veal cutlets on top of the tomatoes and bake for 10 to 15 minutes, until the veal is cooked. Serve with polenta. Serves 4

polenta

1 tablespoon salt
250 g (9 oz) polenta
45 g (1/2 cup) freshly grated Parmesan

To make the polenta, you'll need a large heatproof bowl that will sit over a large saucepan. Fill the saucepan two-thirds with water but make sure the base of the bowl will not touch the water. Bring the water to the boil. Pour 1.75 litres (7 cups) boiling water into the bowl, add the salt and polenta and whisk continuously for about 4 minutes, until the mixture thickens. Cover the bowl tightly with foil and sit the bowl over the saucepan of steadily boiling water. After 20 minutes, remove the bowl, carefully lift off the foil and thoroughly stir the polenta. Cover again and return to the heat. Do this every 20 minutes. The polenta should be ready after it has cooked for 1 1/2 hours. Stir in the Parmesan.

glazed salmon with warm broccolini

80 ml (1/3 cup) mirin
80 ml (1/3 cup) soy sauce
2 tablespoons grated ginger
2 tablespoons red miso
2 teaspoons sugar
2 teaspoons lemon juice
4 x 175 g (6 oz) salmon fillets, skin on
oil, for greasing
185 g (1 bunch) broccolini

dressing
125 ml (1/2 cup) soy sauce
125 ml (1/2 cup) mirin
2 teaspoons sugar

to serve
1 teaspoon black sesame seeds
steamed rice

Stir the mirin, soy sauce, ginger, miso, sugar and lemon juice together in a bowl until combined. Put the salmon in a shallow dish, pour the mixture over it and marinate in the fridge for at least 15 minutes and up to 1 hour.

To make the dressing, bring the ingredients to the boil in a small saucepan, then reduce the heat and simmer for 10 minutes, or until syrupy or like thin caramel.

Heat the grill. Remove the salmon from the marinade and place with the skin side down in a lightly oiled, non-stick, ovenproof frying pan. Cook under the hot grill for about 7 minutes, or until the fish is still pink in the centre and is nicely coloured.

While the salmon is cooking, steam or blanch the broccolini for 2 minutes, or until tender but still bright green and crisp. Sprinkle the salmon with the black sesame seeds and drizzle with some of the dressing. Serve with the broccolini and steamed rice. Serves 4

rare roast beef fillet with roasted tomatoes and mustard cream

1.5 kg (3 lb 6 oz) centre-cut beef fillet
sea salt
freshly ground black pepper
2 tablespoons olive oil
250 g (1 bunch) watercress

to serve
roasted tomatoes (below)
mustard cream (below)
mashed potatoes

Preheat the oven to 240°C (475°F/Gas 8). Season the beef fillet with salt and pepper. Heat a large frying pan over a high heat and add the oil. When very hot, sear the beef on all sides until browned, then transfer to a roasting tin. Roast the beef, allowing 7 minutes per 500 g (1 lb 2 oz) for rare, and 10 minutes per 500 g (1 lb 2 oz) for medium beef. Remove from the oven and allow to rest in a warm place, covered with foil, for 7 minutes.

Pick the leaves off the watercress and discard the stalks. Cut the meat into thick slices and serve with the watercress, roasted tomatoes and some mashed potatoes. Drizzle with pan juices and serve with mustard cream. Serves 4

roasted tomatoes

4 ripe tomatoes, sliced in half vertically
sea salt
freshly ground black pepper
2 garlic cloves, finely sliced
20 g (1/4 cup) fresh breadcrumbs

2 tablespoons finely chopped fresh flat-leaf
  (Italian) parsley
2 tablespoons extra virgin olive oil

Preheat the oven to 200°C (400°F/Gas 6). Arrange the tomatoes with the cut sides up in a small roasting tin. Season with salt and pepper and sprinkle with garlic slices. Stir the breadcrumbs and parsley together in a bowl. Scatter over the tomatoes and drizzle with olive oil, then cook for 45 minutes.

mustard cream

1 tablespoon Dijon mustard
125 ml (1/2 cup) crème fraîche or sour cream
1 teaspoon lemon juice

sea salt
freshly ground black pepper

Place all the ingredients in a bowl and stir to combine.

pork medallions with pineapple salsa

4 pork medallions
2 tablespoons oil
sea salt
freshly ground black pepper

to serve
pineapple salsa (below)
steamed rice
fresh coriander (cilantro) sprigs

Brush the pork with oil and season liberally with salt and pepper.

Heat a large frying pan over a high heat for 2 minutes until very hot. Sear the pork for 1 minute on each side, then reduce the heat to medium and cook for 4 to 5 minutes longer on each side, or until cooked through and golden.

Remove the pork from the pan and leave it to rest for 2 minutes. Serve with pineapple salsa, rice and coriander sprigs. Serves 4

pineapple salsa

350 g (2 cups) chopped fresh pineapple
1 fresh red chilli, seeded and finely diced
2 tablespoons lime juice
1 tablespoon sugar
1 tablespoon fish sauce

Stir all the salsa ingredients together in a bowl to combine.

lemon chicken with a warm lentil salad and herb relish

1 lemon, finely sliced
125 ml (^{1}/$_2$ cup) extra virgin olive oil
4 chicken supreme (breast fillet with wing
    attached, with skin on)
sea salt
freshly ground black pepper

to serve
100 g (3^1/$_2$ oz) baby English spinach leaves
warm lentil salad (below)
herb relish (below)

Mix the lemon and olive oil in a bowl, add the chicken and coat well, then cover and marinate in the fridge for at least 1 hour. Preheat the oven to 220°C (425°F/Gas 7). Heat an ovenproof frying pan (large enough to hold all the chicken) over a high heat. Season the chicken with salt and pepper, place with the skin side down in the pan and sear until golden on one side. Turn the chicken over and cook for another minute to seal the chicken.

Put the pan in the oven and cook the chicken for about 10 to 12 minutes, until the chicken feels firm to touch. Remove from the oven and allow to rest for 5 minutes before slicing the chicken on the diagonal into three pieces. To serve, put a handful of spinach leaves onto each plate, spoon some lentil salad on top, then divide the sliced chicken among the plates. Serve with fresh herb relish. Serves 4

warm lentil salad

1 teaspoon wholegrain mustard
60 ml (^{1}/$_4$ cup) extra virgin olive oil
1 tablespoon red wine vinegar
215 g (1 cup) lentils du Puy, cooked to
    instructions on the packet and drained
^{1}/$_2$ red onion, finely diced

1 teaspoon chopped fresh tarragon
1 teaspoon chopped fresh sage
1 teaspoon finely chopped fresh flat-leaf
    (Italian) parsley
sea salt
freshly ground black pepper

Whisk the mustard, olive oil and vinegar together in a small bowl until combined. Combine the vinaigrette in a bowl with the warm lentils, red onion, herbs and salt and pepper.

herb relish

1 tablespoon salted capers, rinsed, squeezed
    dry and chopped
1 anchovy fillet, chopped
3 spring onions (scallions), finely sliced
3 tablespoons finely chopped fresh flat-leaf
    (Italian) parsley
2 tablespoons finely chopped fresh chervil or
    tarragon
^{1}/$_2$ teaspoon grated lemon zest

60 ml (^{1}/$_4$ cup) extra virgin olive oil
1 tablespoon lemon juice
a few drops of red wine vinegar
sea salt
freshly ground black pepper

Stir all the ingredients together in a bowl, then leave for 1 hour to allow the flavours to develop.

You can use this risotto as a base for other flavours — try replacing the zucchini with canned tuna, or even a mixture of seafood. When using seafood I like to omit the Parmesan.

baked risotto with zucchini, tomato and parmesan

2 tablespoons extra virgin olive oil
1 onion, finely chopped
1 teaspoon sea salt
180 g (1 cup) arborio rice
375 ml (1 1/2 cups) chicken stock or water
400 g (14 oz) can chopped Roma (plum) tomatoes
3 zucchini (courgettes), finely sliced
60 g (2 1/4 oz) freshly grated Parmesan
freshly ground black pepper
2 tablespoons finely chopped fresh flat-leaf (Italian) parsley
shavings of Parmesan, for serving (optional)

Preheat the oven to 200°C (400°F/Gas 6). Heat a 3 litre (12 cup) capacity ovenproof dish (with a lid) over a medium heat. Add the olive oil, onion and sea salt and stir for 5 minutes, or until the onion is soft and translucent.

Add the rice to the dish and stir for another minute. Add the stock or water and the chopped tomatoes and bring to simmering point. Stir in the zucchini and sprinkle with Parmesan and black pepper. Cover the dish and bake the risotto for 30 minutes, or until the rice is cooked. Scatter parsley over the top, sprinkle with Parmesan shavings if desired, and serve in the dish. Serves 4

Shave Parmesan just before serving, using a vegetable peeler. I always use Italian Parmesan, either Grana Padano for cooking, or the top of the range Parmigiano Reggiano for just eating.

ravioli with fresh herb dressing

a handful of green beans
1 kg (2 lb 4 oz) fresh ricotta ravioli
fresh herb dressing (below)
a handful of fresh basil leaves, for serving
shavings of Parmesan, for serving (optional)

Bring a large saucepan of salted water to the boil, add the beans and cook them for 2 minutes. Scoop them out, refresh in cold water and slice them all in half lengthways. Add the ravioli to the saucepan and when the ravioli float to the top, scoop them out with a slotted spoon and put them in a large bowl with the herb dressing. Stir lightly to combine, then divide among four serving bowls. Top with basil leaves and Parmesan. Serves 4

fresh herb dressing

20 g (1 cup) fresh flat-leaf (Italian) parsley leaves
30 g (1 cup) fresh basil leaves
25 g (1 cup) English spinach
1 garlic clove
125 ml (1/2 cup) extra virgin olive oil
3 tablespoons lemon juice
salt
freshly ground black pepper

Place all the ingredients, except the salt and pepper, in a blender and pulse briefly until just combined and smooth. Season with salt and pepper.

cannelloni with fresh tomato sauce

500 g (1 lb 2 oz) ricotta
20 g (^{1}/4 cup) freshly grated Parmesan
2 tablespoons finely chopped fresh flat-leaf (Italian) parsley
1 teaspoon finely chopped fresh oregano
2 tablespoons finely chopped fresh basil
2 eggs, lightly beaten
sea salt
freshly ground black pepper
8 fresh lasagne sheets
2 tablespoons olive oil
80 g (8 slices) prosciutto (optional)
25 g (1 oz) butter, melted
basil leaves, to garnish (optional)

fresh tomato sauce
60 ml (^{1}/4 cup) extra virgin olive oil
3 garlic cloves, finely sliced
sea salt
500 g (1 lb 2 oz) ripe tomatoes, peeled, seeded and chopped
freshly ground black pepper
1 tablespoon fresh basil, shredded

Preheat the oven to 200°C (400°F/Gas 6). To make the cannelloni, stir the ricotta, Parmesan, herbs, eggs, salt and pepper together in a bowl until combined.

Cook the lasagne sheets in a large saucepan of boiling salted water until *al dente*. Transfer the sheets to a bowl filled with cold water and the olive oil. When the lasagne sheets are cool, drain and place on a tea towel. Place a slice of prosciutto lengthways on each piece, then place 2 tablespoons of filling on top. Roll neatly into a tube shape. Brush half the melted butter in a 20 x 35 cm (8 x 14 inch) ovenproof dish and place the filled cannelloni in a single layer in the dish. Brush the remaining butter over the cannelloni. Bake for 25 minutes, or until puffed and slightly crisp.

While the cannelloni are cooking, make the sauce. Pour the olive oil into a saucepan over a medium to high heat. When the oil is hot, add the garlic and sea salt and stir for 10 seconds. Add the chopped tomatoes and stir. Season with pepper. Cook for 10 minutes, or until the tomatoes just start to collapse and form a sauce. Remove from the heat and stir in the basil.

To serve, cut the cannelloni in half and pour the sauce over the top. Some whole basil leaves can be used as a garnish if you wish. Serves 4

parmesan-crusted blue-eye and braised potatoes with peas

75 g (1 cup) fresh breadcrumbs
45 g (1/2 cup) finely grated Parmesan
sea salt
freshly ground black pepper
2 eggs
125 g (1 cup) plain (all-purpose) flour
4 blue-eye or other firm white fish fillets
1 tablespoon olive oil
25 g (1 oz) butter

to serve
braised potatoes with peas (below)
fresh mint

Mix the breadcrumbs, Parmesan, salt and pepper in a bowl. Crack the eggs into a bowl and beat lightly together. Place the flour and some salt and pepper in a bowl. Dip a fish fillet in the flour, then in the egg and, finally, in the breadcrumb mixture. Continue until all the fish is coated. (This can be done in advance if you wish. Cover and refrigerate for up to 2 hours before cooking.)

Heat the olive oil and butter in a large non-stick frying pan over a medium to high heat. Add the fish and cook gently for about 2 minutes on each side, turning once, until lightly golden. Do this in two batches if your pan is small.

Divide the potatoes among four shallow bowls, sprinkle with mint leaves and serve with the fish. Serves 4

braised potatoes with peas

8 kipfler potatoes, peeled and steamed until tender
1 tablespoon olive oil
1 white onion, finely sliced into rings
155 g (1 cup) green peas
250 ml (1 cup) chicken stock
15 g (1/2 oz) butter
sea salt
freshly ground black pepper

Slice the potatoes into discs. Heat the olive oil in a medium saucepan over a medium heat and fry the onion until soft, but not brown. Add the peas and toss well. Add the chicken stock, bring to the boil and simmer for 5 minutes. Add the potatoes and cook for another 2 minutes. Remove from the heat, add the butter, salt and pepper and stir to combine.

roast chicken with roasted potatoes and tomatoes

1 lemon, rinsed and dried
1.5 kg (3 lb 5 oz) free-range chicken, rinsed and dried
sea salt
freshly ground black pepper
fresh sprigs of oregano

to serve
roast potatoes and tomatoes (below)
lemon halves
fresh bay leaves

Preheat the oven to 220°C (425°F/Gas 7). Roll the lemon over a hard surface, pressing down on it, then prick it all over with a fork or skewer.

Season the chicken inside and out with the salt and pepper. Place the lemon and oregano in the cavity, then truss the chicken with kitchen string.

Place the chicken with the breast side up in a baking dish and roast for 15 minutes. Pop the potatoes in the oven. Reduce the oven temperature to 200°C (400°F/Gas 6) and cook for another hour, or until the juices running from the chicken are clear. Allow the chicken to rest for 10 minutes before carving. Serve, garnished with bay leaves and lemon halves, with the roasted potatoes. Serves 4

roasted potatoes and tomatoes

1 kg (2 lb 4 oz) potatoes, peeled and cut into wedges
4 tomatoes, cut into wedges
1 red onion, cut into wedges
50 g (1/2 cup) finely grated Parmesan
2 tablespoons olive oil
125 ml (1/2 cup) chicken stock or water
2 tablespoons fresh oregano leaves

Toss everything together, then put in an ovenproof dish and bake at the same time as the chicken for 1 hour, stirring occasionally.

To get clams to spit out any grit they might have hidden in their shells, put them in a bowl of cold water with some oats or polenta.

linguine with clams and tomatoes

400 g (14 oz) good-quality Italian dried linguine
60 ml (1/4 cup) extra virgin olive oil
3 garlic cloves, finely sliced
2 small fresh red chillies, finely chopped, or 1/2 teaspoon dried chilli flakes
sea salt
1 kg (2 lb 4 oz) clams
125 ml (1/2 cup) white wine
500 g (1 lb 2 oz) cherry tomatoes, cut into halves
3 tablespoons finely chopped fresh parsley
freshly ground black pepper

Cook the linguine in a large saucepan of rapidly boiling, salted water, according to the manufacturer's instructions, until *al dente*.

While the pasta is cooking, heat the olive oil in a large frying pan over a medium heat. Add the garlic, chilli and sea salt and cook gently for 1 minute. Add the clams, white wine and tomatoes. Cover the pan and cook for 3 minutes, or until the clams open. Remove from the heat.

Drain the pasta and add to the frying pan with the parsley. Gently toss to combine, then season with salt and pepper, to taste. Serves 4 to 6

grilled sirloin steaks with wild rocket and rosemary potatoes

4 sirloin steaks, about 2.5 cm (1 inch) thick, 250 g (9 oz) each
2 tablespoons olive oil
sea salt
freshly ground black pepper
4 large handfuls wild rocket (arugula) leaves,
    or normal rocket (arugula), shredded, rinsed and dried
60 ml (1/4 cup) lemon juice
2 tablespoons extra virgin olive oil
rosemary potatoes (below)

Remove the steaks from the fridge and allow them to come to room temperature — this makes the cooking times much more accurate. Brush the steaks with olive oil and season liberally with salt and pepper. Heat a large frying pan over a high heat for 2 minutes. Sear the steaks for 2 minutes on each side, by which time they will be done if you like rare steak. Continue cooking over a medium heat for 1 to 2 minutes on each side for medium and 2 to 3 minutes on each side for well-done.

Remove the steaks from the pan and allow to rest for 5 minutes in a warm place. While the steaks are resting, put the rocket, lemon juice, olive oil and a little salt in a bowl and toss to combine (there is no need to add pepper as rocket is peppery enough!). Divide the rocket among four serving plates. Put the steaks on a chopping board and cut each into thick slices, keeping each one together, then place on top of the rocket, pouring any escaped juices over them. Add some rosemary potatoes to each plate. Serves 4

rosemary potatoes

1 kg (2 lb 4 oz) potatoes, cut into 2 cm (3/4 inch) dice
3 tablespoons extra virgin olive oil
2 tablespoons chopped fresh rosemary
sea salt
freshly ground black pepper

Preheat the oven to 200°C (400°F/Gas 6). Place the potatoes, olive oil and rosemary in a bowl and toss. Place the potatoes in a single layer on a baking tray and bake for 1 hour, or until crispy. Don't stir them for the first 40 minutes, then gently loosen them with a metal spatula. Transfer to a serving plate and season with salt and pepper.

chicken skewers and tomato salad

750 g (1 lb 10 oz) skinless chicken breast or thigh fillets, cut into 3 cm (1¹/4 inch) cubes
60 ml (¹/4 cup) extra virgin olive oil
4 garlic cloves, crushed
60 ml (¹/4 cup) lemon juice
¹/2 red onion, cut into 4 wedges
sea salt
freshly ground black pepper

to serve
4 pitta breads
olive oil
125 g (¹/2 cup) plain yoghurt
1 teaspoon ground paprika
tomato salad (below)

Soak eight skewers in water so they won't burn during cooking. Put the chicken, olive oil, garlic and lemon juice in a bowl, stir to combine, then cover and marinate in the fridge for at least 1 hour.

Separate each onion wedge into three pieces. Assemble the skewers by alternating the chicken with onion pieces on each skewer. Sprinkle liberally with salt and pepper. Heat the grill to high. Grill the chicken for 10 minutes, turning and basting with extra marinade halfway through cooking. When just cooked, remove from the grill.

Brush the pitta breads with olive oil and place under the grill until just warmed through.

Place the yoghurt in a small bowl and sprinkle with paprika.

To serve, distribute the kebabs, pitta bread, yoghurt and salad among four plates. Serves 4

tomato salad

2 tomatoes, cut into wedges
3 spring onions (scallions), chopped
5 g (¹/4 cup) fresh flat-leaf (Italian) parsley leaves
1 tablespoon lemon juice
grated zest from 1 lemon

Stir the tomatoes, spring onion, parsley and lemon juice and zest together in a bowl.

pan-fried fish with spicy green salad and sweet and sour dressing

60 g (1/2 cup) plain (all-purpose) flour
1 teaspoon sea salt
4 firm white fish fillets such as snapper
60 ml (1/4 cup) oil

to serve
spicy green salad (below)
sweet and sour dressing (below)
4 lime cheeks

Stir the flour and salt together in a bowl. Add the fish and turn to coat well. Heat the oil in a large non-stick frying pan over a medium to high heat until hot. Add the fish and cook for 2 minutes on each side, or until the fish is cooked, turning just once.

Serve the fish topped with spicy green salad. Pour sweet and sour dressing over the top and serve with lime cheeks. Serves 4

spicy green salad

2 large fresh red chillies, seeded and finely sliced on the diagonal
15 g (1/2 cup) fresh coriander (cilantro) leaves
12 fresh mint leaves
4 French shallots, finely sliced
20 snow peas (mangetout), blanched and finely sliced
2 fresh kaffir lime leaves, finely sliced

Toss the chilli, coriander and mint leaves, shallots, snow peas and kaffir lime leaves together in a bowl.

sweet and sour dressing

2 tablespoons soft brown sugar
2 tablespoons sugar
2 tablespoons fish sauce
2 tablespoons lime juice

Stir the sugars and 2 tablespoons of water in a small saucepan over a low heat until the sugars have dissolved. Continue to cook over a medium heat until lightly golden. Remove from the heat, add the fish sauce and lime juice and stir to combine.

chocolate self-saucing pudding

125 g (1 cup) plain (all-purpose) flour
a pinch of salt
120 g (1/2 cup) caster (superfine) sugar
3 teaspoons baking powder
4 tablespoons cocoa powder
250 ml (1 cup) milk
85 g (3 oz) unsalted butter, melted
2 eggs, lightly beaten
1 teaspoon vanilla extract

topping
185 g (1 cup) soft brown sugar
2 tablespoons cocoa powder
250 ml (1 cup) boiling water

to serve
thick (double/heavy) cream

Preheat the oven to 180°C (350°F/Gas 4). Sift the flour, salt, sugar, baking powder and cocoa powder into a bowl. Add the milk, butter, egg and vanilla extract and mix with beaters until combined. Pour into four 250 ml (1 cup) greased pudding moulds.

To make the topping, stir the brown sugar and cocoa powder in a bowl to combine, then sprinkle it over the pudding batter.

Pour boiling water carefully over the puddings, then bake for 20 to 25 minutes. Serve with thick cream. Serves 4

You can make the meringues in advance and store them in an airtight container for up to a week.

meringue with fresh cream and blueberries

4 egg whites
a pinch of salt
250 g (1 cup) caster (superfine) sugar
300 g (2 cups) blueberries, hulled and sliced
300 ml (10^{1}/$_{2}$ fl oz) cream, whipped

Preheat the oven to 120°C (250°F/Gas ^{1}/$_{2}$). Place the egg whites and salt in a clean, dry bowl and whisk until soft peaks form. Add the caster sugar, 1 tablespoon at a time, whisking until a glossy, stiff mixture forms.

Spoon out eight meringues onto a baking tray lined with baking paper and bake the meringues for 1^{1}/$_{4}$ hours. Remove from the oven and allow to cool.

Top each meringue with blueberries and serve with cream. Serves 8

lemon mousse

finely grated zest from 3 lemons
60 ml (1/4 cup) lemon juice
185 g (3/4 cup) caster (superfine) sugar
4 eggs, separated
150 g (51/2 oz) unsalted butter, cut into small pieces

to serve
lemon madeleines (below)

Put the lemon zest and juice, sugar and egg yolks in a double boiler and cook over a low heat, stirring constantly for about 10 minutes, until the mixture coats the back of a spoon. Whisk in small amounts of butter at a time. Remove from the heat and allow to cool.

Whisk the egg whites in a clean, dry bowl until stiff peaks form.

Fold half of the beaten egg whites into the lemon mixture with a metal spoon, then fold in the remaining egg whites. Divide among four serving glasses and refrigerate until firm. Serve with lemon madeleines. Serves 4

lemon madeleines

5 eggs
200 g (7 oz) caster (superfine) sugar
finely grated zest from 1 lemon
200 g (7 oz) plain (all-purpose) flour, sifted
1 teaspoon baking powder
180 g (6 oz) unsalted butter, melted and cooled

Preheat the oven to 200°C (400°F/Gas 6). Whisk the eggs and sugar together until they are pale and fluffy, then mix in the lemon zest. Add the flour, baking powder and butter and fold everything together. Leave the mixture to rest for 5 minutes. Spoon the mixture into a greased madeleine tray and bake for 8 to 9 minutes or a little longer, depending on the size of the holes in your madeleine tray.

Peaches come either as clingstone or slipstone (freestone) types, the latter arriving later in the season. You can remove the stone cleanly with a slipstone and they lend themselves much better to recipes that call for sliced peaches.

peach melba

4 peaches
500 g (2 cups) caster (superfine) sugar
150 g (1 punnet) raspberries
1 tablespoon lemon juice

to serve
vanilla ice cream

Score a cross on the base of each peach. Put the sugar and 1 litre (4 cups) of water in a saucepan and bring to the boil over a high heat. Reduce the heat to low and add the peaches. Simmer for 5 to 10 minutes until the fruit is cooked (I prefer the peaches slightly firm). Remove the peaches from the syrup, allow to cool, then peel.

Increase the heat to high and reduce the syrup by half. Put the raspberries in a blender with 4 tablespoons of the syrup and the lemon juice and blend until smooth.

To serve, place a peach in each serving dish, add a scoop of vanilla ice cream and drizzle sauce over the top. Serves 4

champagne jelly with fresh white peach salad

6 gelatine leaves
250 g (1 cup) sugar
560 ml (2¹/4 cups) Champagne
4 white peaches

Soak the gelatine leaves in cold water for 5 minutes, or until softened. Meanwhile, heat 250 ml (1 cup) of water and the sugar in a medium saucepan over a medium heat, stirring occasionally until the sugar is dissolved.

Squeeze out any water from the gelatine leaves and add the leaves to the sugar syrup. Stir until the gelatine is dissolved. Stir in the Champagne, then pour into eight 125 ml (1/2 cup) glasses or moulds, cover with plastic wrap and chill for at least 10 hours, until firm.

Blanch the peaches in boiling water for 20 seconds, then refresh in cold water. Peel and slice each peach, then arrange on a serving plate.

To serve, dip the glasses or moulds in hot water for a few seconds. Place a plate on top and invert the jelly. Serve immediately with the peach salad. Serves 8

You can serve each pudding with fresh passionfruit pulp scooped into the middle.

passionfruit puddings

20 g (³/4 oz) unsalted butter
125 g (¹/2 cup) sugar
40 g (¹/3 cup) plain (all-purpose) flour, sifted
65 g (¹/4 cup) passionfruit pulp
185 ml (³/4 cup) milk
2 eggs, separated

to serve
passionfruit pulp (optional)

Preheat the oven to 180°C (350°F/Gas 4). Beat the butter and sugar in a bowl until well combined. Add the flour, passionfruit, milk and egg yolks and mix to combine. Whisk the egg whites in a clean bowl until stiff peaks form. With a large metal spoon, fold half the egg white through the mixture, then fold in the remaining egg white. Pour into four greased 185 ml (³/4 cup) ovenproof dishes and bake for 12 to 15 minutes, or until the top is golden and puffed. Serve immediately as the puddings deflate quickly. Makes 4

If you use a good-quality chocolate such as Callebaut, Valrhona or Lindt for this recipe it will make the sauce especially delicious.

berries with white chocolate sauce

175 g (6 oz) good-quality white chocolate, broken into small pieces
170 ml (²/3 cup) cream
500 g (4 cups) mixed fresh berries

Put the chocolate and cream in a heatproof bowl over a pan of simmering water. Stir until the chocolate has just melted, then remove from the heat and pour into a jug.

To serve, divide the berries among four shallow serving dishes and pour white chocolate sauce over the berries at the table. Serves 4

chocolate brownies with ice cream and warm chocolate sauce

370 g (2¹/2 cups) caster (superfine) sugar
80 g (²/3 cup) cocoa powder
60 g (¹/2 cup) plain (all-purpose) flour
1 teaspoon baking powder
4 eggs, beaten
250 g (9 oz) unsalted butter, melted
2 teaspoons vanilla extract
200 g (7 oz) dark chocolate buttons

to serve
warm chocolate sauce (below)
good-quality vanilla ice cream
cocoa powder, for dusting (optional)

Preheat the oven to 160°C (315°F/Gas 2–3). Stir the sugar, cocoa powder, flour and baking powder together in a bowl. Add the eggs, melted butter and vanilla extract and mix until combined. Mix in the chocolate buttons. Pour into a lined 22 cm (9 inch) square tin and bake for 40 to 45 minutes.

While the brownie block is still warm, cut it into eight pieces. Place on serving plates with a scoop of vanilla ice cream. Dust with cocoa powder if you like, then serve with the chocolate sauce. Serves 8

warm chocolate sauce

125 g (4¹/2 oz) dark chocolate, chopped
185 ml (³/4 cup) cream

Put the chopped chocolate and the cream in a heatproof bowl and place the bowl over a saucepan of just simmering water. Whisk occasionally until a thick sauce forms. Cool slightly before serving.

Cherries have a short season so don't worry about using other kinds of fruits. Sliced poached pears, or sliced fresh plums or peaches, would be just as delicious.

rustic cherry tart

frangipane

75 g (2¹/2 oz) unsalted butter, chopped
90 g (¹/3 cup) caster (superfine) sugar
80 g (³/4 cup) ground almonds
2 egg yolks
¹/2 teaspoon vanilla extract

1 sheet puff pastry
1 egg yolk
300 g (10¹/2 oz) cherries, pitted and cut in halves
sugar, for sprinkling
cream, for serving (optional)

To make the frangipane, mix the butter, sugar, ground almonds, egg yolks and vanilla extract in a food processor until combined. Refrigerate until chilled.

Preheat the oven to 200°C (400°F/Gas 6). Put a baking tray in the oven to heat.

Lay the puff pastry on a piece of baking paper on another baking tray. Trim off the edges of pastry (this makes the edges rise evenly). Using the point of a sharp knife, and being careful not to cut right through, score a 1 cm (¹/2 inch) border around the edge of the sheet of puff pastry. Prick the entire surface with a fork and brush with egg yolk. Spread the frangipane evenly over the pastry within the scored area. Place the cherries, with the cut side up, in a single layer on top of the frangipane. Place the tart on the hot tray and bake for 15 minutes. Sprinkle with sugar and bake for another 5 to 10 minutes, until the sides are golden and puffed. Serve with cream if you wish. Serves 12

warm apricot pie

filling
1 kg (2 lb 4 oz) apricots
125 g (1/2 cup) caster (superfine) sugar
1 teaspoon vanilla extract
25 g (1 oz) unsalted butter, cut into small pieces
2 teaspoons caster (superfine) sugar, extra, for sprinkling

pastry
250 g (2 cups) plain (all-purpose) flour
2 tablespoons caster (superfine) sugar
180 g (6 oz) unsalted butter
5 tablespoons iced water

to serve
ice cream

To make the filling, cut the apricots in half and remove the stones. Place in a bowl and toss with the sugar and vanilla extract.

To make the pastry, process the flour, sugar and butter together in a food processor until the mixture resembles coarse breadcrumbs. Add the iced water and process until the pastry forms a ball. Wrap the dough in plastic wrap and refrigerate for at least 30 minutes.

Preheat the oven to 200°C (400°F/Gas 6). Roll out the pastry to a 32 cm (13 inch) circle and place in a greased circular or rectangular pie dish, allowing the pastry to drape over the sides. Place the apricot filling on the pastry and dot with butter. Fold the draping pastry over the top of the filling, leaving some parts exposed. Brush the top of the pastry with cold water and sprinkle with sugar. Bake for 45 minutes, or until the pie is golden and the filling is bubbling. Serve with ice cream. Serves 6 to 8

It is really important to not leave the stove for this recipe — you don't want scrambled eggs!

chilled zabaglione

6 egg yolks
90 g (1/3 cup) caster (superfine) sugar
185 ml (3/4 cup) Marsala
finely grated zest from 1 lemon
1/2 teaspoon vanilla extract
185 ml (3/4 cup) cream, lightly whipped

to serve
savoiardi (Italian sponge finger) biscuits (optional)

Whisk the egg yolks, sugar, Marsala, lemon zest and vanilla extract in a heatproof bowl over a saucepan of simmering water for about 5 to 6 minutes, or until the mixture is light and frothy. Remove from the heat and allow to cool. Fold in the lightly whipped cream, then pour into four glasses or a serving dish. Chill for at least 2 hours.

Serve with savoiardi biscuits if you wish. Serves 4

bill's library

Being a self-taught cook, reading cookbooks has been the way I have developed my skills and fuelled my passion for food. I owe all of these great writers many thanks for past, present and future inspiration.

Alexander, Stephanie, *The Cook's Companion*, Penguin Books, Melbourne, 1996

David, Elizabeth, *Elizabeth David Classics*, Grub Street, London, 1999

Dupleix, Jill, *New Food*, William Heinemann Australia, Melbourne, 1994

Dupleix, Jill, *Old Food*, Allen & Unwin Pty Ltd, Sydney, 1998

Hazan, Marcella, *The Classic Italian Cookbook*, Papermac, London, 1980

Hazan, Marcella, *The Essentials of Classic Italian Cooking*, Macmillan London Ltd., London, 1992

Roden, Claudia, *The Food of Italy*, Vintage, London, 1999

Roden, Claudia, *Mediterranean Cookery*, BBC Books, London, 1987

Solomon, Charmaine, *Encyclopedia of Asian Food*, William Heinemann Australia, Melbourne, 1996

Time-Life, *The Good Cook Series*, Chief Consultant Richard Olney, Time-Life Books, Amsterdam, 1978–1982

Waters, Alice, *Chez Panisse Café Cookbook*, HarperCollins Publishers, New York, 1999

Wells, Patricia, *At Home in Provence*, Kyle Cathie Limited, London, 1998

Wells, Patricia, *Bistro*, Workman Publishing Company, New York, 1989

Wells, Patricia, *Trattoria*, Kyle Cathie Limited, London, 1993

Wolfert, Paula, *The Cooking of the Eastern Mediterranean*, HarperCollins Publishers, New York, 1994

Wolfert, Paula, *Mediterranean Cooking*, HarperCollins Publishers, New York, 1994

Wolfert, Paula, *Mostly Mediterranean*, Penguin Books, New York, 1998

index